INFLUENCE

THE SEVEN FACTORS OF SWAY

JB Zegalia

Llumina
Press

ISBN: 978-1-62550-501-9

INFLUENCE
THE SEVEN FACTORS OF SWAY

TABLE OF CONTENTS

TABLE OF CONTENTS

INTRODUCTION

How many times have you bought something and regretted it a short time later? How many times have you woken up the next morning in a panic because of a recent action?

The fact is many of our decisions do not make sense. Many will be made under the influence of the controlling factors of the time. Factors such as emotion, time pressure, persuasion, ritual, and others. While we may feel our decisions are rational in the moment, our reasoning is often brought into play only afterward, when we manipulate the facts to justify the decisions we have already made.

As we will soon see, the decision making process is not always what it seems. We are often placed, persuaded, or emotionally directed in our actions, and our ability to stop or alter a decision is often limited by the circumstances we face. Unlike animals and machines, we are not controlled by instincts or programs; we are often swayed. Good or bad, like it or not, we are not always in control. Even the governing members of our societies throughout history know we are often less culpable for our actions than we pretend to be. First degree murder entails a stiff penalty, but a crime of passion often garners a lesser punishment.

The decisions we make and the factors that drive them are about more than just how or what we do. Everything we are or become is based on how well we are able to influence others, or how we ourselves are influenced. Everything. Influence is where we live, how we live, what we achieve, and what we do not. It is how we accept fate or how we break out and create our own destiny.

There are seven factors of influence that sway us in the decisions we make. And while these factors often affect us before we realize it, a preliminary understanding or awareness of them may help us in better deciding our paths. People who just get by will often only recognize what's on the surface. True people of influence however will either understand or look to further understand these additional factors. That is the purpose of this book. It is an outlined reference of the seven human factors that initiate decisions and actions. Within each factor will be selected stories, experts opinions and direct explanations; all designed to help you best shape the factors when influencing others and yet also to create an awareness in the intended influences from them.

PERSUASION

Persuasion occurs when one person or entity directly influences another. This person or entity may be a salesperson, a politician, your spouse, a governing society, or even a radical group of extremists. It may be for *good* or *evil* purpose.

There are several methods used by influencers to actively persuade others. For instance, the need for a cause or for the acceptance of others who seem in some way attractive or compelling, can powerfully motivate us and make us vulnerable to the persuasion of others. While persuasion is the only factor of influence that is not derived from our own actions, it is still one that we can identify and diffuse.

During active persuasion, an influencer is likely to influence a person using the threat of pain or the promise of reward. We may be motivated or deterred to do as the influencer asks by different levels of each.

What is it that would make you run faster? Being chased by an attacker, or hearing the cheers of a crowd as you race around a track? What drives you? Is it the fear of loss or the desire for gain? The key to influencing ourselves is to understand what motivates us. The key to influencing others is to understand what motivates them.

Two key elements in persuasion are visualization and the ability to adapt. First, we visualize the outcome we seek to manifest, and then we adapt our methods to the specific cause, using techniques that will work with the person we are trying to influence. Much of the persuasion we experience and the influence it garners is both a legitimate and beneficial use of power. Sometimes, however, similar methods can be used in entirely illegitimate ways.

PATTY HEARST AND THE SLA

On April 15, 1974, at 11:42 a.m., the Symbionese Liberation Army entered the Hibernia National Bank in San Francisco, California. The group, along with its new member, "Tania," burst in yelling, "On the ground, motherf...ers. This is a robbery." Four minutes later, with almost ten thousand in cash and two innocent by-standers wounded, Tania and her comrades tore away from the scene.

A month later, two members of the SLA, Emily and Bill Harris, were shoplifting at Dan's Sporting Goods in California. A scuffle ensued when the store owner tried to apprehend them as they were attempting to steal an ammo case. Tania was sitting alone outside in a van. She emerged when she saw the scuffle and fired a series of warning shots over their heads. "Let them go, you motherf...ers," she yelled, "or you're all dead." The group then eluded capture by stealing one car after another.

Only a couple of months earlier, "Tania" had been known simply as Patty, the daughter of publishing magnate Randolf Hearst.

Patty was born on February 4 and grew up in a wealthy part of San Francisco. She went to the Crystal Springs School for Girls in the elite bay area of Hillsborough and to Santa Catalina School in Monterey. She did well in school, and other than being from a successful family, she was a normal young girl. She loved her parents and appreciated the life she led. She displayed no tendency toward trouble and was even a little on the conservative side. For example, she once broke up with an early boyfriend because he smoked pot and she did not want to associate with that element. But soon that would all change.

While sitting with her then future husband, Steve Weed, in her apartment, nineteen-year-old Patty Hearst was abducted by the SLA.

Now taken and changed, one could only ask: How could this girl, one so grounded in her peaceful world, so orderly and correct in her habits, be willing to take part in the acts she did? How is it that any degree of persuasion could lead her so far astray?

A month after the Dan's Sporting Goods incident, the police had a location for a possible SLA hideout. One hundred highly trained officers of the LAPD launched an attack at 1466 Fifty-Fourth Street. As TV cameras rolled, the officers demanded that the residents come out with their hands up. The only response was a burst of automatic gunfire; and because of the extensive arsenal of weapons the SLA had accumulated, the members were, for a while, able to hold the police at bay. The tide soon turned, however, when the police launched a series of tear-gas grenades that started a fire that consumed the house. In the end, six members of the SLA were killed.

Emily Harris, Bill Harris, and Patty, however, were not among the dead. They were now on the run. Patty, while in hiding, became even more vocal. She chastised the media for disparaging her "beautiful brothers and sisters" who had perished in the attack. She declared that out of the ashes she "was reborn."

One year later, on September 18, 1975, with her guard down, Patty Hearst was arrested outside an apartment in the Mission District of San Francisco. While she remained defiant, still pledging her allegiance to her comrades, her parents assembled the lawyers.

Two years from the date she had been kidnapped, Patty Hearst was charged with armed robbery for her participation in robbing the Hibernia National Bank. Her teams defense was that she had been brainwashed and therefore was not a willing participant in her actions.

Despite the prosecution's multiple attempts to settle the case with the promise of a lesser charge, her attorneys, perhaps believing they couldn't lose, stayed the course. But the prosecution was very thorough in its presentation. The prosecution's witnesses and "experts" were quite influential.

Perhaps the most damning testimony came from government psychiatrist Joel Fort. He questioned the ability of other psychiatrists to draw conclusions regarding Patty's state of mind fifteen months earlier. He further cautioned the jury to be skeptical of psychiatrists, as they often wanted to treat individuals as patients rather than criminals. He also suggested that Patty was a prime candidate for radicalism, even before her kidnapping. You see, he had a theory, aptly named the "Velcro theory." According to this theory, an aimless soul would float in moral space until it bumped into and stuck to the first random ideology it found. Fort then insinuated that Patty was a bad kid and offered some "horrifying" examples, such as how she once lied to get out of a test.

As the trial proceeded, at least according to all the accounts found, it began to seem that actual guilt or innocence, armed guerilla or innocent victim, were of little importance. What appeared to matter the most was how effective the opposing teams of attorneys were at influencing the twelve people in the jury. There seemed to be no shortage of professionally trained and recognized experts who were willing to debate the point of whatever side they were on. They were all trained and similarly accomplished, yet when they took the stand, they were somehow able to spout views that were diametrically opposed.

After an extensive review of the proceedings, one could almost picture a new case of brainwashing; only this time, the attorneys played the part of the SLA and the jury played the part of Patty. In the end, Patty and the jurors fell victim to the better persuader. As a result, Patty became a guest of the state.

In its day, Patty's story generated a lot of interest. It seemed that every media outlet was discussing her claim of being brainwashed. The *Saturday Evening Post* chose to uncover and offer a possible explanation. It presented a major editorial review in which it interviewed a number of military groups that surmised that the foundation of Patty's story could in fact hold water. Through the interviews, the *Saturday Evening Post* found that even those who initially resisted could be susceptible to sharing the ideologies of their captors. The paper put together a list of the typical steps involved.

1   Confinement under inhuman conditions to lower resistance.
2   Relentless demand on the confession of past misdeeds.
3   Manipulating the confessions into the context of the ideology where the confession becomes self-criticism.
4   Informing the person their former society had turned against them.
5   Granting "undeserved" liberties commensurate with the person's conversion, which makes the person grateful to the captors and more willing to conform.

6   Continue a weakened physical state to better allow a feeling of shame and inferiority to merge into a bond with the captors.

7   Demanding the captor prove their sincerity by using the same tactics on their fellow prisoners.

8   Repetition, to where even upon returning to society, the person will experience confusion and doubt.

Patty was broken. She was kept in a closet and blindfolded for fifty-seven days. She was made to feel guilty about her privileged past and was told her parents had refused to pay the ransom the SLA had demanded. Her previous thoughts were wiped clean. She was ready for the new ones.

Many believe a major point to understand here is, brainwashed or not, lost in space or searching and willing, the SLA had found a weakness. As stated in the opening, the desired acceptance of another is a powerful motive in one's compliance. It is a vulnerability that human nature has dictated upon us. The same vulnerability that will help make one susceptible to the persuasion of another. When someone sees and is somehow attracted to some aspect of another, an initial interest is sometimes all it takes to start down the path of their persuasion. For the professional influencer, we can only hope their intentions are of good purpose. For the "influencee," we can only hope they have either the opportunity or the awareness to make his or her own sound choice.

The Symbionese Liberation Army used active persuasion to turn Patty into one of their own. They used the threat of pain and the promise of pleasure, as well as the same visualization techniques that work for legitimate causes, but they used them without regard for individual rights. By ruthlessly influencing and brainwashing Patty, without concern for who she was or what she wanted, they were able to use her for their own ends. The same of course has been done before to millions of people. Active persuasion, when used with evil intent, can be a source of destruction and horror; sometimes even to the despair of the entire world.

THE MONSTER WITHIN

Adolf Hitler is considered one of the most polarizing figures who ever lived. As the leader of Germany, his Nazi forces systematically killed into the millions. He led a group of followers who, without a doubt, carried out the most atrocious acts in modern history. Only his designated "kind" were safe. An estimated six million Jews alone were killed by torture, gas, and starvation in the Holocaust. If we include the Romani gypsies, leftists, Soviet prisoners of war, Polish and Soviet civilians, people with disabilities, Jehovah's Witnesses, and other political and religious opponents, the total number of victims is somewhere between eleven and seventeen million people. Never mind the victims who actually died in the fighting.

Hitler's SS soldiers, the command group of his force, led tortuous crusades that often carried out unthinkable, face-to-face acts. They heard their victims' screams, tasted their blood, and endured the incredible stench of rotting flesh as they carried out their "work."

But it was not Hitler who actually committed these acts. Hitler, it's said, never even visited the largest concentration camp, Auschwitz. He did not personally kill millions of people; it was the people he influenced who did.

Hitler's rise to power netted him approximately one million followers, a number too large, in anyone's estimation, to be discounted as those of the criminally insane. Sure, there are people in history and in the present who are morally corrupt. Certain people do not have the moral compass or chemical makeup to exist in the world without incident. But because of the sheer size of his following, you would have to conclude that many of the people caught up in his campaign were "normal" everyday people.

So one has to ask, how could a normal person look into the eyes of another human being, one who has been mentally and physically beaten, and still turn on the gas?

In mass war, an airplane pilot can drop a bomb and never see his victims. Deep below the surface of the sea, a sub commander can flip a switch and see nothing but dots on a screen. Even a sniper does not have the contact with his victims that will necessitate seeing them as humans with souls. There is no immediate threat, emotional consequence, or necessity to feel the nature of their acts because they don't kill their victims face-to-face. And yet Hitler's followers, through a direct channel of influence, were able to ignore any previously instilled sense of mercy or understanding of wrongdoing and brutally murder millions.

Hitler first tried to take power through an overthrow called the Beer Hall Putsch; he failed. He was sentenced to seven years in prison. It was there, while imprisoned, that his method of influence took shape. He wrote his first major work of propaganda, his autobiography, called *Mein Kampf* or *My Struggle*. With this, his direction was set: a direction of speech and propaganda. A direction of influence.

Upon his release, after serving just over a year, Hitler dedicated himself to studying and mastering the skill of persuasion. He sought to understand human nature and learned to manipulate it through disinformation and public speaking. He learned to appeal to a person's sense of belonging and the human need for a common goal. He learned to play on the weaknesses of his audience.

Hitler became a performer. He was a powerful speaker with masterful oratory skills. He took the emotions of his audience and made them his own. He relentlessly prepared for his speeches, orchestrating them from start to finish. When he shopped for clothes, he would try on countless selections, checking in the mirror for just the right "look."

He even had a mannequin built to his likeness so he could see the effect that various hats or outfits would project. He would pose in the mirror for hours to determine the best stance for the image he wanted to create.

Before a speech, he would send his staffers out into the audience to get a feel for the crowd. He often told the speaker who preceded him to anger or humor the crowd, depending on his own preferred opening stance. When speaking to smaller audiences, he learned *who* was in the crowd so he could better relate to them on their level.

When speaking, he would identify with the pain and anger his audiences felt, and then build on it. His "performances" followed a pattern. He would first voice his audiences' concerns, creating a bond with them. Then he would propose a common enemy that could be blamed. He would finish with his "solution." Thus leading his audiences every step of the way. It is said that he hypnotized his audiences, providing the emotional impact needed to enrage them.

Hitler was quite intuitive at understanding the emotional makeup of the human psyche. And as fate would soon have it, the final piece he needed to fully rise to power was rapidly developing around him. You see, Germany had fought a hard war in World War I, and as a result, its economy was heading downward. Growing unemployment, fewer opportunities, and an even bleaker future were starting to take their toll on the people. There was a feeling of unrest and discontent throughout the country. The Germans were a proud people looking for a cause; they were vulnerable. And, as Hitler saw, they were ripe for the picking.

Little by little, he seduced his country with fiery rhetoric and the promise of a "kingdom." His speeches were so powerful that women swooned. His passion, whether real or created, which has often been debated, was nevertheless undeniable. It's been said that once, as a dinner guest, on being challenged, he stood up and screamed for a full half hour, spewing the wrath of his belief.

In the presidential election held on March 13, 1932, Field Marshal Paul von Hindenburg received 49.6 percent of the votes. Hitler received 30.1 percent. Two others shared the remaining percentage. Because Hindenburg did not receive a majority, a runoff election was held, this time with Hitler receiving 36.8 percent of the votes and Hindenburg 53 percent, declaring him the winner. In the following months, Hindenburg appointed Franz von Papen as chancellor. Upon his appointment and unhappy with the current house of leaders, Papen dissolved the Reichstag, the national congress, and called for new elections.

By this time, Hitler had attracted a rapidly growing crowd of supporters. The more he spoke, the more people followed. On the twenty-seventh of July, just four days before the new elections were held, Hitler spoke to over a hundred thousand people in the cities of Brandenburg and Potsdam, and he addressed another hundred thousand at the Grunewald Stadium in Berlin, with a similar number listening outside.

The election at the end of July was a major victory for Hitler's National Socialist Party, winning 230 seats and making it Germany's largest political party. On the basis of the results, Hitler asked to be appointed chancellor. He was denied. So he continued his campaign, using influence and leverage.

With continued chaos and deadlock in the Reichstag, and a lack of ability to provide unity, Hindenburg fired Papen and appointed General Kurt von Schleicher as chancellor. But von Schleicher was also unable to secure a majority or settle the unrest and vacated the post a few months later. Less than a year after the initial election, Hitler was appointed chancellor.

Barely a month later, the final and pivotal piece that Hitler needed fell into place. The Reichstag, where the majority of Germany's leaders assembled, caught fire. In the aftermath, as could be expected, blame was loudly voiced and fear was everywhere. Hitler, understanding the laws of human nature, took full advantage of the fear. He saw what the German people needed and promised them security and structure. Hitler immediately persuaded Hindenburg to declare a suspension of all civil liberties. Then, two weeks after the fire, amidst the fear and unrest, Hitler requested that the Reichstag temporarily suspend its powers and give them to him. With 441 votes for, and only 88 against, Hitler had the majority he needed to suspend the constitution.

On March 23, 1933, as a result of his relentless active persuasion, and the supporters it gained him, Adolf Hitler became the dictator of Germany. He was now free of all constitutional and legislative restraints. He was also free to enact his plan.

Okay. Looking back, can we all say that they should have seen it coming? Can we also say that a similar event could never happen again?

Times may change, but what about human nature? We now have history to look back on, and a lot more safeguards in place, but we should still ask: How often does an influencer find a seeker to influence? How many recent elections, both local and national, were won or lost based on the economic conditions of the time or on a politician's oratory skills? How many times were we sold a great story and, before we realized it, got something we didn't expect?

In bad times, it is natural to vote for change. In good times, it is natural to stay the course. It seems that our actions are almost always influenced by our emotions; and our decisions almost always follow the leader who most vividly visualizes the fulfillment of our desires. Even today, the influencer always finds a home in the town of discontent. And as you know, human emotions can turn on a dime.

Perhaps our only hope is to pray that our charismatic and skilled leaders harbor only good intentions because, even with today's democracy, the resisting 49 percent still has to accept the judgment of the other 51 percent.

FIND AND PROVIDE THE MISSING PIECE

All great influencers look for what's missing in their followers lives, what they yearn to have. Influencers then seek to provide their followers with the belief that fulfillment is possible. Fear, desire, the need for human interaction, the need for one's doubts to be soothed, and the promise of future security are just some of the natural wants that people have. It seems that everyone, in some way, is a victim to human nature. And we all seem to have the emotions that can make us vulnerable to outside influences. Some may be more or less vulnerable than others at certain times; however, the possibility for error or impulse is there. Our upbringing, our fellow peers, our chemical makeup, our emotional stability at the time, and, of course, our influencer's ability to sway us all shape how receptive we are to persuasion.

David Koresh, Adolf Hitler, and Jim Jones are just a few of the leaders who excelled at influencing. They also shared the same determination and dedication to their craft. It is said that David Koresh, the leader of the Branch Davidians, could quote the Bible as if he were reading it. Jim Jones, while growing up, relentlessly studied the lives and traits of Karl Marx, Joseph Stalin, Mahatma Gandhi, and Hitler.

Like Hitler, Jones and Koresh did not seize power. They grew their followings from nothing, one person at a time. They also became skillful at recruiting and training other influential people, which helped to rapidly grow their followings.

Jim Jones and his followers ended their lives in Jonestown, Guyana, in 1975 by drinking cool aid laced with cyanide poison. Over nine hundred people took their own lives, or were murdered, depending on how you look at it. But it could have been worse. Jim Jones was a popular individual. He had contact with prominent local and national politicians. At one point, a member of the California State Assembly and future mayor of San Francisco served as master of ceremonies at a dinner for Jones, which was also attended by the then governor of California and his lieutenant governor.

One political leader, whom you may know from Sean Penn's Oscar-award-winning portrayal, was so impressed with Jones after a visit to his temple that he wrote him a letter: "Rev Jim, it may take me many a day to come back down from the high I reached today. I found a sense of being that makes up for all the hours and energy placed in a fight. I found what you wanted me to find. I shall be back. For I can never leave."

David Koresh's power of influence was so strong that his followers ignored any desires for their own safety and stood by their leader as they burned alive.

For 51 days Koresh and his fellow Branch Davidians ignored the governments requests to surrender and barricaded themselves within the confines of Mount Caramel Center, their compound. Koresh, the leader of the religious group, was wanted for questioning in a series of abuse allegations. Although the federal negotiators treated the situation as a hostage crisis, a two hour videotape was sent out in which the adults and older children explained clearly and confidently why they chose of their own free will to remain with Koresh.

Jim Jones's family suffered from the economic difficulty of the depression that necessitated his family move to Lynn Indiana where he grew up in a shack without plumbing. His father was an alcoholic and he was known as being a weird kid. However, he was also a weird kid with a strong desire to study the religious and political leaders of the past. The probable turning point in his ability to amass a following came when he witnessed a faith healing service at the Seventh Day Baptist Church. He noticed that it attracted people and their money and concluded that with the financial resources from such healings, he could help accomplish his social goals. He would soon organize a religious event where he recruited an already established religious leader to headline the proceeding. He then formed his own church, the Peoples Temple Christian Church Full Gospel.

David Koresh's childhood was described as lonely. He never met his father and was given up by his mother at the age of four to temporarily be raised by his grandmother. Due to his poor study skills and dyslexia he was put in special education classes. After reportedly suffering through his childhood, he would soon begin to sing and play his guitar for some local churches and clubs. He quickly found that this attracted followers and created the desire for more. He then found that studying the bible enabled him to appear more prophetic when he spoke of its virtues.

A major fact that is often missed in the study of these people is that they did not initially seem to be evil. In fact, they were actually seen as good people, even as saviors to some. They were people who had others' best interests in mind, and they offered a "genuine" portrayal of their best wishes. This further emphasizes the potential power of one's ability to sway, and one's potential for acquiring this ability. As just stated, these people were not born persuasive. In fact, in analyzing their early histories, they showed no indications of the abilities they would soon acquire. Nor did they have the privileges that would enable an easy path. What they did have, however, was the necessary ingredients: a burning desire to succeed, a willingness to learn from the knowledge of others, and an impassioned "need" to practice their skill.

THE CREATION OF INFLUENCE

The creation of influence is a process. First, an influencer must understand the individual who needs persuading; then the influencer offers a benefit to persuade that individual. It is a step-by-step progression that discovers a desire and presents a potential fulfillment. It means understanding the likely path to gaining an individual's acceptance. It is understanding someone so they will in turn understand you. Hitler sought the frustrated. David Koresh sought the spiritually misguided. Jim Jones sought the underprivileged.

One has to understand that it is all too easy to look back and judge. But what really must be understood is that one can only see what there is to be seen. For example, while Jim Jones often spoke of the virtues of the gospel, he chose to conceal that his gospel was really the gospel of communism. He'd learned not to present more information than a person could or would accept at a time.

Of course, the moral of this chapter is that anyone can learn the ability to influence others. The more you learn, study, and practice, the more persuasive you can become. This chapter is not a history lesson about Hitler or Jim Jones. It's about how a person, through dedicated study, can gain the ability to influence others. If Hitler can do it, so can you.

BOOT CAMP

In any form of influence, the first step is to clear the way for a new way of thinking. Before you are able to acquire new things, actual or tangible, you must first make room. Whether your goal is to influence yourself or someone else, you must first allow or prepare for a likely acceptance.

The reason many will not allow a new influence to direct their path, is because they are still attached to their current path. The reason our customers will sometimes not close is because they cannot let go of their previous demands. The reason our friends will not consider our point of view is because they're still clinging to their own.

In many cases, people will also not consider a new position until they are in some way able to see the downside or limitation of their present one. Of course this revelation can come from within, or it can come from an outside source. Sometimes all it takes is a simple explanation to make someone see a downside or limitation. Other times however, it may take some preparation. For example, just telling a veteran alcoholic to stop drinking is not likely to be effective. It sometimes takes a process.

The military understands this as well. If possible, they prefer to only recruit people of a certain age. This, however, is not just due to their physical capabilities. Armies want younger recruits because of their lack of mental maturity. You see, as psychiatrist Joel Fort pointed out during Patty Hearst's trial, the military is looking for "wandering souls" too. Individuals who are less set in their ways are easier to influence, making it easier for the military to create the soldiers it wants. The less information someone has, the more likely that individual will have room for more. The more an individual's information is limited in its history, the more likely it can be erased.

Because of their younger ages, most recruits' beliefs are relatively new; therefore they are more easily reconditioned. That is the purpose of boot camp; to break new recruits, to get them to clear their heads. Then the military supplies them with new information that will encourage them to fight and discourage them from dissenting during the fight.

According to widely accepted research, the current plan for new information to be instilled in soldiers is as follows:

1. Create the idea that they are fighting to correct the evil of their enemies.
2. Make them understand that they are helping to protect their fellow soldiers.
3. Make sure they know that they are helping to protect the homeland by removing the threat of outside forces.

All of which seem to make pretty good sense to me, don't you think? So, in this case, even though recruits are "reconditioned" and actively influenced, we as a specific group of society see this as a legitimate use of power.

REHAB

Not only can we be influenced by others; we can also help to influence ourselves. For example, how else could we ever free ourselves from some of the possible addictions that hurt us? Whether it's alcohol, drugs, sex, gambling, a particularly destructive personality, poor food choices, or a way of living, it's sometimes hard to regain our freedom. However, starting with our own initial desire, the allowing of another's help or guidance can make it easier. This is why people often seek the help of known specific methods to get help from things like addiction. Besides the reliance on a "higher power" that is usually a part of these programs, others who have succeeded help us believe we too can take a stand against our weakness.

To break free of an addiction, a powerful plan is sometimes needed. And some are pretty powerful. One such plan worth taking a look at is that of Alcoholics Anonymous. It is a set method that offers a twelve-step program, and has influenced many other plans. The purpose of the program is of course to help create the influence that will allow an individual to overcome their flaw.

As I understand the program, it is a step by step plan to get us to understand our vulnerability to temptation;

and allow for a greater power to help aid us in our struggles. The program requires us to openly admit to our addiction and to accept responsibility for our actions. This enables us to learn from our past and to clear the slate for a new future.

Here is a rough listing of a typical program for recovery or "release." Please note the process of the steps.

1. Admission – First, you must admit that you are sometimes powerless; you are not always in control. Recovery can only begin when we can admit our weaknesses.

2. Trust – Allow for a belief that a greater power can help to restore a sense of sanity. Before we can believe that something can help, we must first trust that it can.

3. Release control – Next, you must turn your will over to a higher authority. All can be corrected if we can release our control to the guidance of something greater.

4. Accountability - Perform a search from within. This is where we look at our weaknesses and create a moral inventory of ourselves.

5. Admission - Admit your flaws to yourselves, others, and your higher authority.

6. Acceptance - Learn to accept your shortcomings as they are, and desire to let them go, allowing your greater power to take over.

7. Release control - Here, you humbly ask your higher authority to release you from your shortcomings.

8. Will to Correct - Make a list of the people you have wronged and be willing to make amends.

9. Make amends - Directly seek to make amends to those you have hurt.

10. Maintenance - Maintain a commitment; continue to take personal inventory and promptly admit your errors.

11. Making contact - Through meditation and inner focus, understand your direction and discover your higher authority's plan.

12. Awakening - Allow for a spiritual awakening as a result of these steps, and continue to practice them in all aspects of your lives.

There are all kinds and levels of addictions. Of course, it's worse to be addicted to narcotics than it is to be addicted to sugar, caffeine, or shopping. But addictions, in the end, are bad for us and will typically hurt us. It may not be readily apparent how they will hurt us, but they always seem to have a price; so having a method of influence is sometimes essential.

This is an example of a plan that influences with a structure. But, again, two of the key elements in persuasion are visualization and the ability to adapt. The reason I bring this up is to make sure you understand that not every plan or method can be the exact template for every type of influence. It's inclusion here is simply to show that a plan of some sort is often needed to successfully influence. Whether the guidance you desire is for the influence of yourself or of others, you will first have to understand the mechanics of a likely path. You will then have to visualize the influence you seek, adapting the best plan to fit your cause.

BOTH SIDES OF THE TABLE

The creation of influence is a two-way street. Sometimes we will look to influence others, and sometimes we will be on the receiving end. Some we will seek and some will seek us. Fortunately, our understanding of the one will often further our understanding of the other.

The SLA's process, Hitler's, and even the process of recovery, although quite diverse, all have one thing in common. This, of course, is that influence is in fact a process, a process that is created from the understanding of others, and their likely acceptance of influence.

In much of the research available on persuasion, there will often be advice.

The majority of the advice given for accepting influence, if summarized in a few sentences, would be something like this:

For the persuasion of ourselves, we should always look to understand our vulnerabilities in order to avoid or repel unfavorable influences; yet should also allow for the benefit in accepting positive influences.

For the persuasion of others, we must first understand the desires and vulnerabilities of our intended influencee, and then create the perception of benefit in the direction you wish them to take.

When seeking to increase your influence, the best view is a complete view. Influence, and the study of it, is best seen when you can recognize how others are influenced and how you were influenced; both for good and bad purposes. Even if your intentions were of a completely positive nature, it would still make sense to explore and analyze the darker side of another's intentions and their path of choice. The only true potential for good or evil is in one's intent. Knowledge is knowledge. The greater the view and the broader the scope, the better the understanding one can have. Both a positive or negative intent, toward or against, can offer a lesson. With awareness and choice, and of course an understanding of the nature of influence, objectivity can be of one's own choice.

Of course this advice and our earlier stories are just some of the examples for further learning. As I stated earlier, Hitler was not born influential and neither were you. It is an ability only attained from a true desire to become influential and a dedication to learning and practicing your skill. You will have to proactively seek the knowledge and path of others. Fortunately, we have a lot of powerful lessons in history of which to learn.

PLACEMENT

Paralyzed, like a deer in the headlights, the young man did not know his next move. He had never stolen before, but there he was, in the middle of the mall with an armload of Cannon's new lightweight digital cameras. Now that the lights were back on, thanks to the reserve generator, it was time to make a new decision in his "new" environment. *Crazy*, he thought. It all seemed to make a lot more sense just five minutes earlier when the lights suddenly went out. Amidst the excitement and fear, people everywhere began grabbing everything they could get their hands on. But it was okay. There are no laws in a blackout, right?

The looting of New York City is a perfect example of the influence of placement. When the lights went out, it was no longer the same city it had been just minutes before. The blackout temporarily suspended the accountability one would face in the brightness of the light. It also established the speed at which this influence could be felt.

On July 13, 1977, the city of New York went dark. A lightning strike had tripped a number of breakers, and a number of additional strikes, failures, and overloads inexplicably followed. With a set of failing stations and alternate systems falling like dominoes, "Big Alice," the largest generator in New York, went down at 9:27 p.m. By 9:36 p.m., the entire Con Edison power grid had failed.

The blackout occurred in the evening hours, instantly changing the entire cityscape. Although the emotions and underlying unrest that the residents of the city felt carried their own momentum, it was not an emotional force that triggered the events that would soon unfold; it was the resident's new placement in a world gone dark.

Looting and vandalism were widespread. Crown Heights, possibly the hardest hit neighborhood, had over seventy-five stores looted. In Brooklyn, thieves stole over fifty new Pontiacs from a now unprotected dealer. Broadway was in chaos with complete blocks on fire. Over a hundred and thirty of its stores were looted and forty-five of them set ablaze, resulting in thirty-five blocks of the historic district being almost completely destroyed. In the Bushwick section of Brooklyn, a fourteen-block stretch of jewelry, clothing, appliance, and furniture stores all had their contents relocated. In the South Bronx, looters stole $55,000 worth of merchandise from one store alone. Many of the store owners, also compelled to adapt, took up arms to protect their shops. Destruction and violence were hard to avoid with over thirty-one neighborhoods being hit, including every poor neighborhood in the city.

In the aftermath, over 500 police officers were hurt and 3,500 looters were arrested. The city, in its new state, looked like it had been hit by a natural disaster the likes of a hurricane or earthquake. The burnt out stores smelled of smoke and ash, and damaged or unwanted booty littered the streets.

Psychiatrists say that to understand the mind of another, you have to place yourself in that person's position. You have to see from that person's perspective. Well, I believe this can be applied here. The people of the city were no longer in their previous environment, and that gave them a whole new perspective. In a society of rules and repercussions, we are influenced to conform. In a society without rules, we do not have the same sense of accountability.

The Reverend Vincent Gallo, a Catholic priest, said, "When the lights went out, people just said, 'Here's our chance to get back at the mothers who have been ripping us off for years.'" While some chose to resist, many others simply helped themselves to whatever they wanted.

In the midst of the melee, *Time* magazine reported one man yelling, "The lights are going to come back on, but what about the jobs?" Another was overheard saying, "Take your chance, when you get your chance." You see, they evidently understood the law of placement. They realized that the blackout would eventually end and that everyone would at some point be back in their previous city.

Many have argued that some of the residents would have stolen anyway. But any logical calculation of the numbers would overwhelmingly indicate that most chose to participate only because of the new conditions that existed. These people, good or bad, would have normally gone about the business of their regular everyday lives.

But influenced by placement, the looters and arsonists orchestrated events they would never have considered in normal circumstances.

THE DIFFERING DISLAY

A diamond resting in a case at Tiffany's and a similar one placed in the jewelry counter at Sam's Club will never produce the same effect. The one at Sam's Club won't sell for as much or be as appreciated in the same way as the diamond at Tiffany's. Even though the two diamonds may be of equal cut and were formed in the same earth and in the same manner, they are not the same. Even though logical or expert analysis might counter this assessment, it will not matter. Please understand, the influence of placement is more than just perception, it often transcends reality and becomes stronger than actual fact.

Is a shirt bought at TJ Maxx or Marshall's any different from the same shirt at Macy's? Does it matter? Will we ever feel the same about them? No matter how you look at it, we usually feel a little more confident wearing a Macy's shirt as opposed to one bought at a discount store.

Is the warmth or comfort of a designer jacket more real than that of one without the brand name? We know it's not. But if given the opportunity, most any shopper will prefer to wear the designer label. In many cases, it seems, buyers will even choose a brand before other concerns, such as feel, fit, or comfort. These qualities, if considered at all, are likely to be secondary.

As all professional marketers understand, the placement, the display, and even the packaging of an item are often more important to its sale ability than the actual item itself. Yes, "you can't judge a book by its cover," but how often does that really ring true at the time of purchase? Many feel the reason that this is such a popular saying is because people often will judge a book by its cover.

IT'S ALL IN THE VIEW

Placement not only influences our actions, it influences how we perceive our surroundings and how we formulate our thoughts and decisions. Research has shown that the influence of a chosen environment or even a God-given ability or characteristic will likely, justly or not, sway our decision making.

Dr. Lawrence Sanna, professor of psychology at the University of North Carolina, and his team of researchers conducted a study in which they had a person collect charitable contributions at both the bottom and the top of an escalator. Interestingly, the people who rode the escalator up and were asked to contribute at the top were often more generous than those who were approached at the bottom. People, it seems, are often more virtuous or compassionate when positioned in a higher place. As a result of his many studies, Dr. Sanna further suggests that placement is more than just about charitable contributions. For example, the management team of a company may be able to boost the helpfulness of their staff if they can hold meetings on the top floor of their offices. In another example, perhaps more easily relatable to the general population, people might want to consider inviting their friends upstairs before asking for a favor.

Arthur Aron and Donald Dutton performed a study where they found male participants were more likely to be emotionally interested in a woman after walking over a high bridge. In this study, the experimenters staged two events. In the first, a group of men were told to walk across a low and sturdy bridge. In the second, a second group of men were told to walk across a high bridge that was 450 feet in the air and quite unstable. At the end of each bridge, an attractive girl waited, pretending to be a survey taker. She asked a series of questions and then gave the participants her number so they could find out the results. The study found that an overwhelming number of the participants who walked over the higher bridge, over five times as many, called her, showing that the influence of a more precarious environment actually heightened their emotions and ultimately their actions. Then, just to be sure of their findings and to completely determine that the interest of the men was the result of their environment and not related to their personalities, Aron and Dutton repeated the study, but they waited some hours before having the girl interview the participants. When the girl conducted the same survey and offered the same phone number after some hours had elapsed, the percentage of callers went way down.

Dr. Sally Augustin, a recognized environmental psychologist, suggests that higher ceilings may promote greater creativity and innovative thinking. She says that the feeling created in a more expanded room encourages a "big picture" outlook, while lower ceilings are more likely to produce a more personal or intimate perspective. Her research has found that the area around us is a significant factor in the measure of how we relate to others.

Kathleen Vohs, a professor of marketing at the University of Minnesota, has found that sound, both volume and style, will affect how people act in different environments. One example, such as in a typical store, suggests that loud volume may lead to sensory overload, which makes people less able to make a logical decision. Under these conditions, "People might be lured by brand names or fooled by discounts." In other examples, a restaurant may choose to forgo sound absorbing materials for a sound bouncing environment, like one with tiled floors, in order to make the place seem busier. In finer restaurants, they may choose to play slow music, which encourages patrons to hang out longer, maybe for that extra piece of pie or drink. Additional research has found that the style of music may also affect the decision-making process. A French study revealed that playing empathetic music increased tips. And wine store workers noticed that when playing French music, they sold more French wines, and when playing German music, they sold more German wines.

The things you touch in an environment may also influence you more than you know. For example, the weight, texture, and firmness of items in your possession or surroundings will all produce an effect. The research of Joshua M. Ackerman, Christopher C. Nocera, and John A. Bargh, in their article "Incidental Haptic Sensations Influence Social Judgments and Decisions," offers up some cool findings.

According to their research, if you were holding a heavy object while interviewing, you would likely give more seriousness to the person or decision in front of you. For example, if you were holding a heavy clipboard, you would be more likely to give funding to a project you were considering.

Next, they found that smoothness is associated with ease and roughness is associated with difficulty. A treated puzzle was the experiment. Those with the smooth pieces found it easier to relate to the others in their social experience.

Finally, they found that hardness in one's environment meant a firmer stance. In an experiment, they had test customers negotiate for a car. The test customers who were sitting in a firm chair were much less likely to agree to the presented figures. In the study, each person was told to make an offer on a sixteen thousand dollar car. If a person's first offer was rejected, the person's return offer was $350 closer to the person's first one, compared to the people sitting in the soft chairs.

PEOPLE PLACES THINGS

Is a man more likely to be seen as guilty when led into a courtroom in handcuffs than when seen walking to his chair in a suit? Is an attorney's defense more likely to be seen as credible if he is well dressed and surrounded by a large supporting group of lawyers?

While neither would, in itself, make either individual more or less "guilty," placement affects our impressions; and our impressions are often the foundation for our decisions. With further investigation, we have to wonder how many people were found not guilty because they were well "placed" by their character witnesses. Conversely, how often is a defendant thought to be guilty simply because his friends or family attending the trial made him look bad?

Fortunately or unfortunately, depending on its direction of influence, placement, fairly or not, is about more than just where someone is sitting or what bridge he crosses. Placement can be perceived in our names, our race, or even in our physical attributes. Right or wrong, logically or not, people are influenced or may influence others based on how they are placed. A man with a baby face may receive a lighter punishment when convicted of fighting than a man with a rough exterior. And if he were given a lighter sentence, would those people chosen to apply the sentence be consciously aware of the influences that might have affected them?

THE LOCAL AREA GANG

Sometimes, because of the familiarity of everyday life, our perspectives are so swayed that we can actually lose the ability to see things as they really are, or as they should be. We can lose sight of the overall truth or the bigger picture all because of a biased view. But maybe the gang down the street can encourage us to have a new sense of understanding. Let's take a look.

As a society, we agree that things are right or "okay" when the majority of those in our circle of influence think they are. So if something is accepted within our culture, it is deemed as correct or proper. This is true even if the same action is thought of as wrong in another culture. Perceptions of right, wrong, good, bad, weird, or normal are all relative to where we are. The influence of laws, the media, and our peers all lead us to conform. In this way, our placement influences who we are and what we can do.

So, back to the example. When I was younger, I would sometimes hear people say, "I answer to a higher authority." At the time, I thought, *Oh god, one of those people*. Now, at least in the sense of witnessing the power of this influence, I can see a deeper meaning. I think that the word "higher" puts the effects of this influence in a better perspective.

In this example, let's consider the aspects of war. In doing so, I want you to take a second to open your mind. Don't think of yourself as an American or a Frenchman.

Don't even think of yourself as a being of this earth or universe. Clear all your partiality and allow yourself to have no bias at all. Separate your thoughts from your time instilled morals so that you, as the holder of certain thoughts and values, will not be offended. Remember, we are not changing anything here or condoning anarchy. We are just examining the effects of influence.

In most countries, governments set the rules and guidelines by which people live and conduct business. They also protect the rights of their people. In doing so, they set up controls and lookouts at their borders to protect their chosen way of life. They also commission a group, their military, to repel or resist potential threats from outsiders. And within this military, there is a hierarchy of leaders who coordinate their varying duties.

Now, if some entity, say another hierarchy from another country, tried to alter the way we live or conduct business within our borders, we would consider them invaders. It is, after all, our land, our turf, and our rules. Our military is trained to fight other people, to resist the intrusion of others. And during that fight, the military's intent is to take any action necessary to accomplish its goal. This military group, for fighting, might receive medals, awards, and great honor, all for killing members of an opposing nation.

Now. If we were looking down on these events from space, we might ask: What's the difference between a military war and a gang war? Both organizations are protecting their people and their lands. They are both protecting the daily lives of their people and the businesses that they engage in. But where a soldier would be honored for killing a member of the opposition, a gang member would simply be a murderer.

Yes, you might argue the legitimacy of the business being conducted, but what you have to realize is that the business might be legitimate within the particular rules of their societies. For example, gambling is illegal. That is, unless the "higher authority" of that particular society, like the local or federal government, is getting its cut.

This demonstrates the influence of placement. Our thoughts are influenced by our conditioned points of view. Now, ask yourself: Would a real higher authority, say one above our government, view each of these proponents in the same way? Would a true higher authority look at the soldiers as heroes and the gang members as murderers?

Seriously, who's to say the gang members shouldn't be allowed to defend their turf, to resist outside forces from getting in their way? Is the immediate, larger authority of the land correct or justified in its view?

Well, right or wrong, essentially it is. The placement under its authority decides whether people are murderous gang members or valiant soldiers. The winners are honored as heroes and saviors, and the losers are tried for crimes against humanity. Right or wrong, it's all in the placement.

SPRING BREAK, PROM NIGHT, AND VEGAS

The fact that you hold a high GPA, study relentlessly, rarely date, and typically spend more time in the library than the local mall, all mean nothing on your first trip to Florida. It's spring break, and your placement is new, with new rules and new opportunities. As history shows, your new environment, coupled with a desire for emotional release, may encourage an eventful stay. Your actions will likely conform to the atmosphere that your expectations and the other spring breakers have created.

But this is okay, even encouraged. It's human nature. For example, have you ever gone somewhere and come back with an accent? If you did, it means you were just adapting to the social nature of the environment you visited. You were simply "fitting in." Your new actions were influenced by your new placement. A new environment changes the accepted norm, thus, consciously or not, our human nature to conform takes over. Just like the saying, "When in Rome, you do as the Romans do."

Another example is prom night. In this environment, the rules change. They may not even apply. In setting the scenario, mothers will typically instill in their children what it means to be respectful. And dads, especially if they have daughters, are just waiting to kick some young punk's ass for even thinking about engaging his daughter. But on prom night, there are other influences at work. It is special. It almost falls into a type of time warp, where sex is thought to be acceptable or even a right on prom night.

And because it is thought to be more acceptable, you may be influenced to indulge. The night's influence allows you to have fun and retain your self-respect.

They say that what happens in Vegas stays in Vegas. It too is a setting that allows for its placement to influence. For example, stepping out on your boyfriend or girlfriend while in Vegas is often viewed as not really cheating. For some, Vegas is like another dimension. It's a space of time in our lives that, once it's over, never really existed. Although we might have to logically admit that, yes, we cheated; we allow such thoughts to be repressed. Soon we start to believe our own justifications, and eventually yes, we convince ourselves that it never happened. It's like calling a time out during a football game. What happens on the sidelines doesn't happen in the field of play. Our new and distant placement allows us to separate from reality and act differently, differently than we normally would in our hometowns. The freedom to act the way we want without taking responsibility or even acknowledging our behaviors is simply how the influence of placement works.

WHO'S TO SAY THEIR RIGHT AND YOUR WRONG?

Ok now really. When it comes to religion, cultures and greater powers, who's right and who's wrong in their chosen beliefs? Or, simply due to ones placement, can this ever be answered or even agreed upon? Well, let's take a look, and start at the beginning.

A culture is a sector of civilization that has its own distinct beliefs, traditions, religions, and accepted guidelines for behavior. At least, that seems to be the general definition, as "a culture" is difficult to define. The uniqueness of each, however, is not a debated point. Some beliefs will have you knocking on doors, and some will have you sacrificing virgins. Some may encourage you to strap a bomb onto your back, and some may simply encourage you to love your neighbor. If your placement is in India, you may see the cow as sacred. But if your placement is in midwestern America, you are more likely to give thanks for the steak you are about to eat.

Now, ask yourself: How can millions of people be right in their beliefs and virtues and millions of others be wrong?

Religion, often just as difficult to define, appears to have no set number of variants either. Adherents.com lists forty-three thousand citations for the existence of over forty-two hundred religions in our world. Some say less, others claim even more. In anybody's estimation, however, there are many different religions in the world, all with different structures and values.

So who is accurate in their beliefs?

The question this raises is not new. It is also both highly contentious and difficult to answer. A person's belief in a higher guidance and religious stance are often quite sacred. Again, bear in mind, I am not challenging or questioning anyone's beliefs here, I merely want us to investigate the influences that we, as humans, are susceptible. But the question remains. The conclusion given in many religious debates is that, logically, not everyone's beliefs or views can be right; therefore, some must be wrong. But how can this be? Or, more to our point, how can some refuse to even ask? Additionally, how come many cannot, or will not, logically recognize or even consider anothers point of view?

Are some people so influenced by their own beliefs that the idea of another's beliefs angers or upsets them? Is it possible that a Catholic and a Muslim can look at each others' accepted beliefs and without hesitation consider them wrong? Are some groups repulsed by even the thought of some others practices? Well, yes. And many of the few who are curious are self-admittedly scared to even broach the subject. Even more interesting is that the vast majority of people will die believing the same historical and accepted beliefs that their parents taught them from birth. Even faced with countless logical discrepancies and scientific proof, people of all faiths will stick to their beliefs, avoiding or disallowing any other explanations. But let me ask you a question. If you were born in another land, one where your beliefs were not practiced accepted or even known; can you honestly say you would still likely have the same beliefs you presently do?

The moral here, and the relevant lesson for any potential influencer, is that, rational or not, people will believe what their placement has influenced them to believe. Logic may be "logical," but if people don't want to hear your logic, it will have little or no affect on their decisions. There is no amount of proof that you can throw at someone who still lives in their placement or is not ready to change his or her beliefs. The influence of placement profoundly dictates our paths.

However, the point for the influencer or marketer to also understand here is that in your quest to gain or alter a person's view, your success depends on your ability to understand your chosen individual's creation of influence. For example, as seen with those in the blackout, you may have to supply some type of trigger to initiate your desired reaction. As with the visitors to Vegas, you may want to encourage or allow for some type of excuse, or acceptable justification. As with one's own viewpoint, you may want to allow for a view of a bigger picture. Since it is here that a person's placement is the source of his or her influence, the best first step to influence that person's thoughts and actions would be to literally or visually create a new placement. Take your intention to another place to garner the actions you desire a person to take. Create the scene that will best afford you the influence you seek.

Again, though, the creation of influence is sometimes a process. Understand that different people will attach different degrees of importance to each of their individual thoughts. Certain people will be more set in their placement or beliefs, which may cause them to resist the efforts of an influencer. But with gradual persuasion, taking one step at a time, resetting the scene, and never going too far or suggesting more than someone is willing to believe at a time, a person of skill can still find the path for another's acceptance. Learn your skill, understand the participants, and relentlessly practice your technique.

RITUAL

Within minutes of arriving at the scene, the investigators of the San Francisco Police Department were already gathering evidence. One body was face first on the kitchen floor with the obvious red stains so indicative of what a firearm can inflict. Another lay motionless on the also stained, cold clay tile floor of the home's foyer. His legs were comfortably resting slightly tucked up against his body, and his arms were tightly folded in front of his abdomen. It almost looks that he must have been cold, as he took his last few breaths. His body, now slumped against the left side wall, was adjacent to the home's entrance. Both of the victims were Caucasian and appeared to be of middle age. They were well dressed and, other than the obvious, appeared quite healthy.

Arriving at the scene of a double homicide was always a new experience. There would always be new answers to the questions of how, why, and who. What may appear to be inconsequential to some, may be quite telling to others. As each new investigator arrived, they searched for the clues that would help them solve the case. Little by little, they cordoned off the area and tried to visualize how the events had unfolded.

However, other than the two now frozen corpses, there was nothing out of place. There was no sign of forced entry and no indication of a struggle. There weren't even the spent casings that so often littered the floors in most shootings. It appeared that the detectives had their work cut out for them.

Upon lifting the yellow crime scene tape, it was clearly obvious. Detective Adrian Monk, a special consultant and former police detective, had locked in his focus. There were two stacks of magazines on the kitchen table, and one was clearly higher than the other. Although this somehow seemed to elude the other investigators, this lack of balance was like a blaring horn for Mr. Monk. In fact, it was the only thing that existed to him. It was quite obvious what had to be done. Three of the magazines were going to have to be moved from one pile to the other. The key, of course, was to choose the specific three that would total the exact thickness needed. The entire procedure was predicated on the ability to see what others could not. However, this of course was no challenge for a person of Monk's obvious talents.

Ahh, perfect. In less than a minute, and to the disbelief of the gathered crowd, he had perfectly balanced both stacks of magazines. His mind was now free to actually investigate the case.

Adrian Monk, as anyone who has watched the show knows, has obsessive compulsive issues. When things like the magazines bother him, they really bother him. He can't think about anything else or do anything else until the issue is resolved. His sandwiches can't have crusts; his clothes are all identical; he won't shake hands with anybody; and, no matter how outlandish they may seem, his rituals must be observed, regardless of what else is going on in his life. He can't function unless they are.

SPOCK WAS FROM VULCANIA

Our point of course here, as we will further investigate, is that before we can influence someone we must first in some manner gain or allow for their attention. You must see through their eyes. You must realize their present ability to see what it is you want them to see.

Even from the earliest of times, superstitious beliefs and irrational rituals have been prevalent among all groups of people. For example, early Egyptian paintings show that the Egyptians time was largely dedicated to either pleasing the gods or avoiding upsetting them. The Egyptians sought the signs from above to help guide them.

Although the affects of ritual influence the decisions of some people more than others, to some extent, we all have a little ritual in us. We all feel a little more comfortable with some sense of predictability in our lives, even if that predictability is of our own making.

It may not make sense to some, but you may like having the bills in your wallet sorted from highest to lowest, or the fork set to the right of your plate. You may like creating the parallel lines that result from the way you cut your grass.

No? Well, have you ever felt out of whack when something altered your morning routine, or a little uncomfortable when signing the daily receipts without your lucky pen?

What may be acceptable to you might be thought strange by others, and vice versa. Whether we admit it or not, we are all, in some way, guided by our own sense of what is normal and right. And others are guided by theirs. While our "eccentricities" may be curious to some, our routines ground us in a sense of familiarity and acceptance.

Some psychiatrists believe that Americans, as a people, have become so ritualistic that we may have lost some of our objectivity. As a result, we are unable to consciously see where our habits have brought us. We accept these habits, and these habits influence our every move.

THE EYE OF THE BEHOLDER

So, who were the original choreographers of the rain dance? Whose idea was it to sacrifice the first virgin?

What may seem outlandish to you may be deadly serious to others. And, although we may be most familiar with extreme rituals, it is often the lesser, more subtle rituals that have the most impact on our lives and on our ability to influence others.

Before you can expect anyone to make a decision based on your values or beliefs, you must first understand whether or not this is possible for them. You have to know who the person is and be able to recognize how they are guided. Here again, seek first to understand before you seek to be understood. No transference of influence, yours or theirs, will ever be received without understanding the complexities of another.

Is it possible that others might not understand or agree with the beliefs and traditions you hold true? Search for the rituals in your life and see if you can identify how they may influence you.

If you can, try to separate yourself from your body. Picture yourself up in the corner of whatever room you may enter. Follow yourself for a day, a week, or a month. Watch and analyze your moves and actions. Try to imagine how others may see and think about the actions you take. Try to objectively watch yourself as if you were someone else. Try to recognize what might seem strange to others, say someone from a different culture or era.

Is there potential for someone to misunderstand some of the traditions in your culture? Will people respond differently to customs that you find natural, comfortable, and familiar?

Do you participate in the ceremonial Eucharist on communal Sunday? Is being submerged in water essential for your salvation? Do you wear black at a funeral and white at a wedding? Do you cringe at seeing a black cat or rejoice at finding a four leaf clover?

Understand that the thoughts and beliefs that influence you may not influence others. The power and beliefs of our cultures, religions, and accepted authorities are just some of the factors that impact our ritualistic behavior, and ultimately determine how we are influenced.

Understand also that rituals are not necessarily restricted or objective. They are often simply the everyday routines that we, consciously or unconsciously, engage in throughout the normal course of our daily lives. Many of our rituals are a fundamental part of our existence.

For example, most of us have rituals that we use to prepare for the day. We wake up, eat breakfast, take a shower, and put on the clothes that suit our occupation. Our preparation, Monday through Friday, even Saturday and Sunday, may be quite regimented. Every day, and throughout the day, we are creatures of habit, creatures of ritual.

When we arrive at work, we straighten our areas, lay out our tools, and begin our tasks. We get a cup of coffee, greet our coworkers, and turn on our computers. We stop for lunch, and we wait for the clock to tell us to go home. When in America, we greet our guests with a smile; when in Japan, we greet our guests with a bow. Where we eat, what we eat, the routes we take, where we park, and the entrances we enter are all often routine. Familiarity provides the comfort we need.

TWO FLIPS FOR FOOD

In some cases, it appears that these patterns of behavior are just simply hard wired into the electrical charges that a living body may have. Burris Skinner, a professor of psychology at Harvard University, has found that humans are not the only ones that may engage in ritualistic behavior. In his research, he conducted a study to explore the reference of what has happened to what will happen in pigeons. It speculates the irrational belief that performing or acting in a certain way will, in fact, affect the future.

In his experiment, Professor Skinner placed a number of hungry pigeons in cages where an automatic mechanism would deliver food at various, random times. In observing their actions, he soon discovered that the pigeons associated the delivery of food with the actions they were taking at the time the food was delivered.

One bird was conditioned to turn in a certain direction, making two or three turns for its intended result. Another developed a tossing routine where it would lower and then raise its head as if it were flipping an object. Two birds developed a pendulum motion with their heads, swinging back and forth in a quick move followed by a slower return.

This experiment demonstrates how rituals can be created out of random events. The birds behaved as if there was a relationship between their actions and the delivery of their food, though the timing of the deliveries had nothing to do with their behavior.

Now, this whole study may just be for the birds. Unless, of course, you're a golfer. In which case, you know that the last ten feet of a putt requires a certain twisting and contorting from you to help "influence" the ball into the cup. Bowlers do it, too. We might also want to include pool players as well.

IT HAS A NAME

With the recent campaign for its awareness, you will likely be familiar with its attributes. We've all probably seen Monk on TV straightening some picture on a wall, or Howie Mandel from *Deal or No Deal* fist bumping his guests to avoid shaking their hands.

Obsessive compulsive disorder, or OCD, is said to affect about one in fifty people. Milder forms may affect many more. Simply explained, OCD is an anxiety disorder characterized by uncontrollable, unwanted thoughts and repetitive, ritualized behaviors that the sufferer feels compelled to perform. It stems from the irrational belief that any deviation from a ritual can negatively influence reality. Those with OCD only obtain a certain degree of comfort or correctness from the rituals they perform, thus making rituals absolutely necessary. Something cannot be considered okay until some inexplicable authority says it is.

OKAY, BUT I'M STILL GONNA
THINK ABOUT IT

With the recent awareness of the traits of OCD and the ever-competitive need to attract, keep, and understand business, marketers are concentrating more and more on the irrationality of human behavior. And it is because of this awareness that they have begun to explore the subtle ways in which the majority of people are directed.

Understand that a person's rituals or sense of comfort is a major factor in them accepting your influence. Often, when a person wants to think about or sleep on a decision, it's because he or she feels that something is not quite right. The person may not know the source of his or her concern, but the person's subconscious does. The sense of ritual will flash warning lights. This is why potential influencers must first determine the cause of a target's unease before they can start to overcome what may be considered as real or logical objections. They must use an approach that will get to the origin of the person's concern and then bring it out into the open. To do this of course, they cannot limit their search to what may be seen as reasonable.

So. Does it matter if you don't have OCD? After all, you might not. But just to make sure, let's take a look. Without getting too technical, you should know that OCD is the result of an imbalance in certain chemicals in the brain. The chemical serotonin is said to be the main player. Its presence or lack of, and its degree of activity influences the way we think. All our brains use this hormone, and, to some degree, we are all susceptible to its influence. You see, because of outside influences, such as diet, amount of sleep, or level of stress, the amounts and activity of this chemical vary. So our ability to make decisions varies as well.

Regular everyday decisions can be erratically influenced by the moods serotonin creates. A higher state of unease is often brought on by anxiety, which is a natural byproduct of the decision-making process. Anxiety causes indecision. Indecision causes anxiety. So we can become "stuck," which influences us to take irrational actions to relieve the pressure.

The two points that I want to emphasize are these:

1) Like it or not, to some degree we are all influenced by ritual. If you think it over carefully, you will see how you have created some, perhaps innocuous, rituals in your life. We all need some level of predictability and control. And this is established by creating some type of consistency, routine, or ritual that provides comfort. We can't always expect people; customers, friends or associaites, to logically respond the way we want. Because logic will not always bring them the comfort needed to act.

2) Examining the extremes of behavior enables us to recognize that not everything we do makes sense on a logical level. Understanding this is critical in becoming an influencer and in understanding our own acceptance of influence. The study of this allows us to see that life is not just black or white, yes or no. Other factors may be involved, logical or not. One of the keys to creating influence is to first understand the individual you're trying to influence. But if you only look to your own sense of what is a reasonable motive to enact a decision or action, you never will.

ELEVATOR ONE TO LOSE;
ELEVATOR FOUR TO WIN.

On a recent trip to Las Vegas, I naturally tried my hand at gambling. There seems to be quite the opportunity there. On my first trip down to the casino, I took the main elevator. It was an average night. I lost a little, wrote it off to "entertainment," and went on to one of the other available entertainments. The next day I had a similar experience. The following day, because of excessive waiting, I took the elevator across from the previous one I had taken. I won relatively big. A return to the first set of elevators on the next night brought a similar result as it had before.

The next trip down, awareness hit me. It made more sense to take the elevator that had brought me my winning day.

THE POWER OF EIGHT

Different cultures have different beliefs. Here are a few you may find interesting:

In Japan, the number four, like thirteen in America, is considered extremely unlucky. It is also common knowledge that the majority of Japan's hotels and hospitals do not have a room numbered four. Which, of course, leaves me to wonder, if the rooms go one, two, three, five, isn't room number five technically room number four?

Starting with the Romans, it has been considered bad luck to get up on the left side of the bed. Hence the saying, "She must have gotten up on the wrong side of the bed." But don't worry. You can counter the bad luck by putting your right sock on first.

Have you ever "knocked on wood" to avoid bad luck? Do you know why? Well, many early cultures believed that the gods lived in trees. History has it that the first knock meant that you needed good luck. The next two knocks were to say thanks.

Opening your umbrella inside is said to offend the local sun god, and may bring ill fortune or even death to you or your whole family. As you may know, in former times, the umbrella was often used more for protection from the sun than from the rain.

Some unofficial surveys claim that up to half of all professional baseball and poker players engage in some type of ritual before start time.

In China, it is said that the number eight is lucky. It is also said that the phone number 8888-8888 was sold for more than $200,000. So you could say it is more than just lucky. It's valuable.

In some Asian cultures, being in the middle of a picture of three may bring the misfortune that will upend your world. Look, I'm not sure if any of this is true. But is it really worth the risk to find out? If given the opportunity to trade places, to not be in the middle, would you? Shouldn't you?

A cashier from a Quick Mart told me that customers often add another item if their tally comes to a certain three matching numbers. I really don't see the need to list that particular number here, maybe because I'm scared too. But as a hint, I will offer that the number in question is the one just after the number five.

Okay, okay. I know. None of this is real. It's not logical and doesn't make sense in our world.

But odds are, you and your new spouse still brushed rice off your wedding clothes. You know, the tradition where two people devote the rest of their lives to each other in a time honored ceremony. Something old, something new, something borrowed, something blue.

THE POWER OF AWARENESS

In terms of influence, there are generally three groups displaying different levels of perception. Members of the first group have little or no care for their surroundings or the surroundings of others. They simply allow their desires or emotions to dictate their decisions. These people are followers. They are quick, impulsive and often an easy sell.

The members of the second group, where the vast majority of people are, know what they like and have preferences, but they won't try to understand why. The thoughts and images that compel an OCD sufferer may often occur in the subconscious of this group. This group responds to sharp marketing and dismisses less well developed strategies.

The members of the last group, those who are ultra perceptive, are marketers, leaders, motivators, and problem solvers. Members of this group will investigate, wonder, analyze, compare, study, reference, and calculate. They will also create the traffic, get the vote, and make the sale.

Although it may encompass other characteristics, this type of person shares many qualities with the obsessive compulsive. A need for correctness is a leading influence in their understanding. When taking action or making decisions, obsessive compulsives are more likely to be guided by underlying thoughts than they are to be guided by any sense of logic. They have to feel that things are just right, that they've parked in the right spot or double-checked that their doors are locked. They will often ignore certain rationalities and thus better focus on recognizing the underlying factors of others. Their own ritualistic behavior provides an increase in perception. Because everything is a task or decision, these individuals have to evaluate their surrounding influences down to the minutest level. They are able to see subtle attractions and distractions that others do not. They are also more likely to recognize that what might please or bother you will not necessarily please or bother someone else. They understand that it is the small and often irrelevant attributes of an item, a situation, or an environment that can encourage or deter a decision or action.

Of course the point here is that to become a better influencer of others, the study of others and their rituals is essential. People who are more perceptive in these ways make better influencers and even leaders, because they are better at recognizing the wants, needs, and attractions of others. They can be more effective in creating an environment that will attract followers, customers, or even voters. They open their awareness to all potential surrounding factors. This, in the world of marketing and social science is mandatory. By understanding that things do not have to be obvious, or even rational or logical, a person will undoubtedly be better at directing the actions of others.

About one in every fifty people suffers from a specifically diagnosed obsessive-compulsive disorder. One in three, however, have a good-luck shirt. Allow for your awareness.

PAST EXPERIENCE

Past experience is probably the most influential of all factors. That's because it's derived from your own past, not someone else's active or direct persuasion. The image you visualize comes from within; therefore, it is easier for you to accept. The images you visualize may be contrived or misleading, but the history on which you base your decision is not. Nobody has the ability to go back in time and alter your past. Since the source of your reference is not in the present, it cannot be threatened by another's influence.

Past experience is also one of the most controversial influences. This is because the influence we've accepted could affect the future of others.

For our own future, our past experience will directly influence our decisions. Plain and simple. If we touch a hot stove and get burned, we are done. We ain't touching it no more. If we shop for a car and have already owned both a stick and an automatic, our past experience will direct our future ownership. We know what we like. The longer and more encompassing our past is, the more it is filled with experience, the more we are set in our ways, and the more we know what we want. Our years of past experience guide us in identifying and avoiding decisions that will cause us pain or loss, and guide us in making decisions that will give us benefits or pleasure.

That being said, there is also a second aspect to this influence. And this is where the controversy lies. The second aspect occurs when we use our past experience to make decisions about others.

For example, you may feel that the twenty dollar bill you just received is a fake, or the person you just passed on the way out of the store is hiding something that he or she probably didn't purchase. These assumptions are based on the feelings you had in similar past experiences.

This second, more subjective, influence is more controversial because . . . you could be wrong. And this could affect others, not just you. You may also open yourself, your motives, and your ability to read people to outside scrutiny. It will involve the pros and cons of others feelings on intuition, profiling, stereotyping, and even educated guesses. All of which, when combined with different abilities, different situations, different biases, and even different motives, can, as you see, be the source of argument. This is especially true when some form of authority is involved, or where the public can judge such decisions after the fact. For example, if a pilot were to hold up a flight and have a certain passenger removed, the results of an investigation into the incident would either produce a win or a lose situation. If a plastic explosive was found on the passenger, the pilot would be a hero. If all checked out, the pilot would likely be considered a racist.

TIME ON THE JOB

Socially accepted or not, many of the impressions that will influence us will often be automatic. In referencing our past experiences, we will often be able to form accurate visions of our future. Our previous experiences will allow us to make snap decisions about our current ones. And the resulting influence from these experiences can be formed either in our conscious minds, like in a simple comparison, or in our subconscious, like with a more complicated or underlying influence.

An important factor to understand here is that this influence is not only automatic, it's unavoidable. This, I believe, is simply part of human nature. If we see a pattern from the past in our current situations, right or wrong, consciously or unconsciously, we will reference it to influence our future actions and decisions. And we will continue to believe these influences, sometimes even when faced with contradictory evidence. Again, right or wrong, we will be influenced by the images from our past experiences, seen through our initial snap thoughts.

The reason we do this is because we play the odds that established patterns from our past will be indicative of the future. This is similar to how a police officer will make the decision that "someone is up to no good" based on the person's mannerisms or surrounding environment, such as whether the person "fits in" or not.

As with any calculation, we will use the factors or clues we see to guide our decisions. The more our past experiences show consistent results, the more we will base our future judgments on those results. Right or wrong, politically correct or not, we, as a general rule, will be influenced by our past. We can see this from our direct experiences or through influencing others in our past.

REFERENCED

Let's take a minute to understand something here. The immediate cognition of our view is not based on some left field guess. It is not based on an innate trait or a woman's "intuition." It is a legitimate tool of judgment that is based on real past experience. This is what I believe to be the perceived difference between "past experience" and "intuition."

Although the definition of intuition seems to allow for a decision that is and is not backed by past experience, it is too often thought to be where it is not. Some people will discount a person's "intuition" because they feel it is no more than a hunch. In doing so, they unwittingly include the influence of past experience in the same category and discount it as well.

Intuition is probably best described as a summation of our past experiences and our calculable impressions. Although we may not know all the details of how we arrive at a decision, when we draw from the past, our collection of impressions, understandings, and experiences can often provide us with an accurate picture when we need it. Past experience, on the other hand, is more conscious. We know that we like automatic transmissions better than stick shifts because we've driven both, and we know that we need to be careful around a hot stove. We are conscious of these past experiences; they are known to us. Intuition just draws from a bigger pool of past experience, even from experiences we weren't aware had occurred.

MICE DON'T LIE

More and more, as the effect of influence is accepted as a key factor in understanding the decision-making process, marketers and researchers alike have become intent on quantifying this science. One such group has initiated a study on the influence of past experience in mice.

Researchers at the Massachusetts Institute of Technology have recently shown that mice, when performing an action, will look to their past for guidance. Specifically, researchers have found that when mice explore new areas, neurons in the center of their learning and memory areas fire sequentially, essentially igniting a makeshift fuse. By looking at a timed sequence recorded from the firing cells, researchers can tell which part of the maze the animal was running at the time, thus showing that knowledge gained by "past experience" can subconsciously influence behavior in new situations.

In the latter part of 2010, researchers George Dragoi and Susumu Tonegawa found that some of the sequences that fired during a spatial experience, such as running a new maze, had already occurred while the animals were resting before their next experience. Of course, the researchers were unable to determine if the images from the mice's past experiences occurred in their conscious or subconscious memories. Mice may be affected by past experience, but only humans can analyze why.

JUST IN TIME

I found my favorite example of a man drawing from his past experience while reviewing the work of Professor Gerard Hodgkinson of Leeds University. According to the university's website, Professor Hodgkinson is currently a professor of organizational behavior and strategic management. His research in the cognitive studies of strategic decision making is quite extensive and rather illuminating. Here's a paraphrase of the example I'm referring to:

During a race, a Formula One driver suddenly braked before a turn without knowing why. In doing so, he avoided a sure collision with a group of cars that were bound up just ahead. Because of the degree of the turn, he could not have seen the other cars, so it was quite a mystery to all as to how he knew to brake.

After the race, the driver underwent forensic analysis by psychologists. During their efforts, he was shown a video that was meant to help him mentally relive the event. In hindsight, he realized that the crowd, which would normally have been cheering him on, wasn't looking at him, but was looking the other way in a "static and frozen" manner. That was his cue, his picture into the past, as this was a typical crowd reaction to an accident. Thus he was able to stop in time and avoid a collision.

THE MAKING OF A DECISION

I believe that people make decisions frame by frame, like taking a movie reel off a projector and then looking at each image one by one. Each image supplies information and a new impression on which to base our decisions.

I also believe, from a purely logical position, that it makes sense to make quick decisions; *if* the situation in question is one we have previous experience with and if the initial frames provide adequate information. The subconscious mind is powerful and capable of guiding us in proper decision making. The more experience we have, the more likely its influence will guide us correctly.

The potential trouble here, and I believe the true source of the controversy I mentioned earlier, is that some people feel they are qualified to make decisions about or for others when they are not. Their previous experience may be too limited. And because they lack the experience to make correct decisions, they also lack the experience to realize they lack the experience. Basically, you don't know what you don't know.

Having trained salespeople for most of my life, I find it funny when a new salesperson will claim a level of expertise after only a month or two on the job. I, too, when first starting out, experienced a sudden case of expertise at about the same time. This early "experience" can be a problem.

A second issue is that people sometimes hang onto their initial decisions too long. A momentum can occur after an early commitment, even if that commitment is premature. Thus, a lack of experience and momentum together, can produce flawed decisions; some with major repercussions.

MALCOLM

One of the most engaging books about past experience is the popular *Blink* by Malcolm Gladwell. I hope by now you have read it so that some of my further deductions will make better sense. But if you haven't, you still can.

Blink, in Gladwell's chosen words, or "in my estimation" I guess I should say, is about the power of thinking without thinking. It is the ability to instantly and quite often accurately gauge what is important. It is about one's ability to "thin slice" a view to form a "blink" conclusion.

One factor that makes his reading so engaging, at least in my opinion, is that he never really presents a conclusion. He may allude to certain beliefs, but he mostly leaves it up to the interpretation of the reader. For example, he gives the example where one's quick grasp is both correct and incorrect.

The relevance of this to my point is that in the examples he gives, the more "past experience" his subjects had, the more likely they were to be accurate. The more history someone had in a particular field, the more likely that person could see what others couldn't, and the more likely that person was right. That is, as long as the person wasn't in some way "biased" in his or her belief, which I will explore later in this chapter.

THE REAL REASON

As I was pulling out, he was pulling in. It was about eleven thirty at night, and I was on my way to find some type of heater. You see, I was away from where I normally lived. I was working out of town for a sales company and was staying at a local extended-type hotel when, for some reason, the heater in my room quit working.

His quick glance and following U-turn should have forewarned me, but I wasn't worried. I would just drive straight, and he would eventually pull off in another direction. That was how it had played out in the past. As long as you don't give a curious officer any further reason, the officer is unlikely to do more than just follow you.

Anyway, as my light turned green, his lights turned red. When he asked me if I knew why I was stopped, I said no. He said I didn't have a front tag, which was true. In the state I was in, the "dealer" tags were only placed on the back, and the company I was working for had such a tag.

When his second question was "So, when was the last time you were arrested?" I suddenly realized what I was driving. Although I had my choice of cars, this one night, it had just been convenient to take home this particular car. I think one of the gauges on the dash might have shown a favorable condition. Anyway, it was small, inexpensive, and, in my current position I could see, quite old. I then realized how several other things might look: my hooded sweatshirt, the time of night, my younger-looking face, and my departure from the hotel.

His third question, as he looked at my license, was "So, did you know there have been complaints of drug activity at that hotel?" I didn't answer. I didn't because I wanted him to go back to his first question. I had a new answer. "Yeah, I know why you pulled me over. Because I'm young, I look poor, it's late, and, judging from your aggressive manner and the prolonged sweep of your flashlight, you feel pretty confident that I just bought some drugs."

It's kind of hard to explain. Then and even today, I can see each side. In some ways, I get a little mad. In others, I kind of understand his reasoning. There is no doubt in my mind that in that particular instance, I would have had my bet on the same side of the table as he did. I really did fit the profile.

On the other hand, he was wrong. I didn't have any. And his excuse of no front tag was just that. In that state at the time, all dealer tags were quite obvious. Any first-day cop would know this, and he obviously did as well. He knew my registration was on the back of the tag. My biggest mistake, I'm sure, was choosing the car I did.

Because driving while poor, at least in some areas, is just as bad as driving while black. And, as I remember from my own past, pretty close to driving while young.

PROFILING

Profiling, according to dictionary.com, is "the practice of categorizing people and predicting their behavior according to particular characteristics such as race or age." It occurs when we use historical evidence to create what we hope is an accurate guide for the future. It is, in many ways, the very definition of making a decision based on past experience. While it, too, can be a source of controversy, it appears that the public is agreeable to profiling, and many are even staunch supporters of its potential. When not abused for personal motives, profiling has often proved to be an accurate and beneficial influence. Some disagree.

However, whether we admit it or not, we all tend to rely on profiling in our lives. Much as a veteran detective relies on the consistency or lack of consistency in a scene to arouse his suspicion, we, too, may allow for a degree of increased awareness in our own situations.

Many people do not want to believe that they are predisposed to such an influence, but is this really the case? Are we really immune to the pictures from our past? Can we really be objective during the first few seconds when a new image takes form in both our conscious and subconscious minds? Well, let's see.

In the following makeshift little experiment, I want you to read the list of people and scenarios. Take note of the image that appears in your mind. Don't over think here, just allow for an image and freeze. Read each line one by one:

A serial killer.

A terrorist on a plane.

A crack dealer on the street.

An accountant at a computer.

A dentist in his office.

A used-car salesperson from the 1980s.

A librarian sitting at a desk.

A swimsuit model in a hotel.

A CEO giving a speech.

A Martian.

Now, on a conscious level, ask yourself: Are you a racist? Are you a sexist? You may truly be able to say that you are not, but can you also say that you are immune from creating an image that might seem racist or sexist?

If you did create an image, where did it come from? How were you influenced? Was it the news, a personal experience, the voiced opinions of others? Do you think your images might be stronger or weaker based on the amount of previous experience you've had?

Please understand that there is a fine line between accurate and inaccurate profiling. This is simply because there is no foolproof way to correctly analyze a current picture based on a past experience.

But does that mean we should not acknowledge when profiling might be useful? For example, should a marketer make no attempt to adapt his or her store's marketing to the buying habits of the customers that the store attracts? Should a detective not investigate when confronted with a scenario that indicates foul play if a certain racial or ethnic profile is involved? Should a man not hold onto his wallet when approached by an evil swimsuit model? Was the Martian you pictured green? And finally, unless you were born yesterday or came from Mars, can you ever fully separate yourself from the influence of this factor? Careful, nobody likes a hypocrite.

STEREOTYPE

Now, stereotyping is not the same as profiling. Profiling is a behavioral science designed to identify common behavioral, emotional, and psychological characteristics in various types of individuals; much of which is based on statistical analysis. Stereotyping, on the other hand, is derived from conjecture, bias, subjective interpretation, prejudice, and speculation. It is not based on quantifiable research.

Stereotyping, according to the more popular encyclopedias and dictionaries, is the categorizing of a group of people. It is the general typecasting of a segment of society to use as an identifier. It is the grouping of perceived characteristics or actions that does not take into account individual factors. Stereotyping makes standardized and simplified conceptions about groups based on assumptions. These assumptions may be about a group's traits, goals, values, or beliefs.

So why does stereotyping occur? Well, according to these sources, the combining of lesser-known individuals is often due to people's lack of familiarity with the group in question. And, as humans, we do tend to stereotype. This happens, I think, because we come up with pictures or ideas based on our past experiences when we're confronted with new information. We can't help but think about our past experiences when they cross our minds. It's an automatic and unavoidable response to stimuli. But because our need to understand what we see is stronger than our need for accuracy, we often take shortcuts. We do this by skipping further investigation and placing our assessments of the information in the most convenient categories. It's like if you walked down the street and grabbed every image you saw, quickly placing each in a particular basket.

The controversy comes in, first, because our conscious minds can only process so much information at a time; we can only carry so many baskets. And second, because our experience with a particular image may be limited, biased, or incorrect, we could place it in the wrong basket. So we see, we calculate, and we shortcut; therefore, we stereotype.

Another reason people stereotype, I think, has to do with the bonds between the people in the group doing the stereotyping. Stereotyping may allow the group's members to feel better about themselves and make them feel connected to one another with their shared views.

As sensitive as this practice may be, some people, probably more than would publicly admit to, do stereotype others. On the whole, it's a human habit that is difficult to overcome. As a result, it's to be expected that, on occasion, people will say the wrong thing and other people will take offense. A bigger view should also make it apparent that people can take offense to group identification, especially when the group is stereotyped as having demeaning or derogatory traits.

ACCURATE INFORMATION

The best way to process our images can often be found through our current communications. But our communications can often contain hidden motives or agendas. Because of this, we need to be able to "read" people and situations accurately before we can allow the images from our past to align with our current ones. In doing so, our two most effective abilities are the ability to read someone and the ability to filter out someone's misleading responses. After all, the only way to truly understand people is to receive accurate information.

First, let's take a look at lying. We might lie to save someone's feelings or to add a little zest to a story. Whatever the reason, we, and the people around us, are not always truthful. The ability to exaggerate or color the truth is often learned at an early age, and as we grow, we get better at it. The more lies we tell, the better liars we become.

To help recognize the misleading, we will first take a look at the eyes. As the saying goes, the eyes are the windows to the soul. They are our connection to the outside world, and the world's connection to our inside world. The eyes receive information and provide it to others. This is because they are our quickest link to our thoughts.

As you probably know, there are two sides or hemispheres to our brains: the left and the right. The right side is our random, intuitive, creative side. The left side is for sequential, logical, and rational thinking. Even more interesting, the right brain governs the left side of the body and the left brain governs the right. Knowing this, we can see that the following makes sense.

When we look up and to the right, we are using the left hemisphere, our sequential, logical side, remembering the story we are telling. Thus, when people look to the right, they are probably being truthful.

On the other hand, when we look up and to the left while telling a story, we are using the right hemisphere, our imaginative side, so we are probably creating the story. In short, we are lying.

Another way to detect a lie also involves the eyes, or at least, eye contact. People who are trying to deceive you will often avoid meeting your eyes. They will look away, so you can't evaluate their words.

Also if people try to create a barrier when they are talking to you, by maneuvering objects to block your view of them, putting their hands in front of their faces, or leaning forward to hide their mouths, this is evidence that they may be lying to you.

In addition, if they are anxious or defensive, they may be uncomfortable with what they're saying. A sudden change in position or a need to roam around may also offer insight. Because lying causes stress, it may be uncomfortable, and demand a change in position.

My favorite way to tell if someone is lying is to quickly change the subject when the person is saying something. If the person is willing to accept this, he or she was probably lying and is relieved to move on. If the person refuses to change the subject, however, the person is probably being truthful, and this would explain the person's desire to prove his or her point. Truthful people believe in what they say, but liars are scared of details and do their best to avoid them.

Deceivers will also often repeat exactly what you say, then simply add a qualifier to deny it. They don't try to be creative, as this may cause them to show their uneasiness or insecurity. They also try to avoid introducing any new information that may dispel their assertions or offer new avenues of detection.

Even something as simple as the use or nonuse of contractions can help us tell if people are lying. People who don't use contractions in their responses are more likely to be lying than those who do. For example, saying, "No, I did not go to the store," shows structured resistance; while saying, "No, I didn't go to the store," shows a calm confidence. People who are lying are not as comfortable as those who are telling the truth. So the natural flow of words can imply truthfulness, while the unnatural flow of words can imply the opposite.

When people speak in a monotone or controlled manner, this may also indicate deceit. Preferring to use only the words needed provides individuals with the structure they feel they need and allows them to think about what they are saying as they say it. Also look for pauses when people speak. Pauses are oftentimes needed for creating the details.

If people omit or refuse to discuss certain parts of their stories, you might want to question them further. We all know that truth may often be found in what's hidden.

Inconsistencies are also indicative of falsehood. If what people say doesn't add up, there may be a reason for concern. It's often difficult for liars to remember all the exact details of their stories, especially when they are making them up as they go along.

READING PEOPLE

The success of any interaction between two people depends on how the two parties act and react to each other. Whether you are selling something, trying to attract someone, seeking guidance, or trying to influence someone, understanding the thoughts, intentions, and desires of the person is critical to your success. Your ability to read a person is a vital skill in shaping a relationship and a key to understanding any situation.

Before we can get someone to accept our influence, we must understand what we are seeing.

The first step in reading people is to observe an individual to develop an overall picture of the person. You will see a collage of impressions that will gradually come together as you recognize patterns and make tentative predictions about behavior. Watch the person's movements and listen to his or her voice. Think about what you are seeing and hearing. Start with an open mind and involve all your senses. Gather information about the person and the setting, collect the clues that will help guide you.

The point here is to develop an image of the individual's personality and emotions so you can know how to best connect. By understanding people's actions and reactions, we can often determine their underlying emotions. By understanding their personalities, we can anticipate their actions and prepare ourselves to respond appropriately.

Knowing how people dress, how they walk, and the company they keep, all provide insight into who they are. Take these observations and combine them with their style of language, tone of voice, and facial expressions. Look for patterns and for how things match up. See if you can pull their overall appearance and actions together and rough out the fundamentals of personality, a starting image. Would you expect a more direct approach from a busy person? Would you be more reserved when trying to connect with a shy person? As your constructed image of the individual evolves, and who the person is becomes more apparent, you can adjust and adapt it, bringing it into focus to create your own response.

When trying to understand a situation, visualizing the presence of a particular individual may help you define it. When trying to connect with a person, creating an amicable interaction allows you to maintain the influence you desire.

A good example of a person's preferred style of contact can be found in how the person relates to his or her friends. If the person of interest is with someone else, pay attention to how they interact. Use what you see and hear as a reference. Try to recognize the common patterns of mannerisms and emotions. Focus on their voices when they speak. In many cases, it is not what people say that is the true message, but how they say it. Where they put emphasis in a sentence, the pitch of their voices, and the rate of their speech will all offer insight into their thoughts, intentions, and future actions.

Does a loud voice indicate someone who needs to be in control? Does fast talking indicate nervousness or falsehood?

Determine whether the person knows that he is altering his voice. Is this his natural tone or is it the result of the emotions he's feeling?

The fastest way to improve your ability to read people is simply to observe. Watch people. The more people you encounter and analyze, the more information you will have for future guidance. The more data you have to draw on, the more likely you'll be able to develop an accurate picture of an individual when the need arises. Create your past experience file.

Focus on people's actions, mannerisms, and speech. Evaluate their emotions and personalities. While watching and listening, look for insights, patterns of actions and reactions, and create a plan. Understand that your ability to read an individual or situation matters. The closer your constructed image is to the reality of the person, the better you will be able to relate to the person, and the more likely you will be able to exert influence over the person.

Once you can effectively observe and understand the situations and people you encounter, once it becomes second nature to read people, your ability to successfully allow the influence of your past experience to create better future decisions and actions will also excel.

EMOTION

In the spring of 1951, Mrs. Yvonne Chevallier received an anonymous letter suggesting her husband, Pierre, was having an affair. During a quick search of his belongings, she found it was true. A signed letter from his lover, discovered in the pocket of one of his suits, left little doubt. Some say his fate was already set.

Yvonne met Pierre in the city of Orleans, France, in 1935. Pierre was a medical student at the hospital in Orleans, and Yvonne worked there as a midwife. He was from a prominent and well established family, and she was the daughter of a farmer. Despite the differences in their social and economic backgrounds, their relationship grew, and four years later, they were married. In 1940, their first son was born. Yvonne was faithful, but the same could not be said of Pierre. He was a handsome man, dashing and debonair, and he soon came to prominence as a leading figure in politics.

In the early 1940s, around the time their son was born, Adolf Hitler invaded France. Pierre participated in the French resistance and was awarded the *Croix de Guerre* and the French *Legion d'Honneur* for his acts of bravery. In the aftermath of the war, he was elected mayor of Orleans. Pierre soon became even more involved in politics and started spending long weeks in Paris.

Despite her husband's drifting attention and rising ambitions, Yvonne stood fast. Feeling his loss of interest, she worked hard to regain his love. She taught herself politics and studied the arts. She invested in more flattering attire and frequented the best beauty salons in town. But the more she was left alone to watch the kids, the further she and her husband grew apart. Yvonne Chevallier was soon an emotional wreck.

The other woman's name was Jeanette. She was beautiful, with striking red hair that complemented her soft, fair complexion. A woman of sophistication, her social status was also closer to Pierre's. Despite being married herself, to Leon Perreau, the owner of one of the finest department stores in Orleans, Jeanette was smitten with Pierre.

After finding Jeanette's note, Yvonne rushed to Paris to confront her husband. But he refused to see her, reportedly having an attendant keep her out of the building where he worked for the National Assembly. On his return to Orleans, he refused to discuss his affair. Well, Yvonne became unglued. She threatened suicide, but to no avail. Her hurt soon led her to purchase a Mab 7.65mm semiautomatic handgun and twenty five rounds of ammunition.

On August 11, 1951, Pierre Chevallier was sworn in to a ministry post in Paris. The next day he was to appear in a town near Orleans. On the way, he asked his driver to stop at his home, so he could change his clothes. After his arrival, Yvonne confronted her husband in his dressing room. She begged for his love. She pleaded with him, promising to "better" herself. He, in turn, was brutal in his rejection. He reportedly brought up divorce and declared his love for Jeanette. His disdain was the last straw. Yvonne quickly left to fetch her new tool of negotiation. She held the gun to her head and threatened to kill herself. Pierre simply laughed, daring her to do it.

Yvonne's first shot caught Pierre square in the chest, surely grabbing his attention. The following three did not miss either. In the midst of this debacle, her son appeared, just in time to see his father gasping on the floor. After leading her son away, Yvonne returned and mindlessly fired her final cry of pain into her husband's dying body.

In court, Mrs. Jeanette Perreau did not deny her affair. She confessed their love had begun in 1950 and had continued until the day of his death. She and Pierre had met as frequently as two or three times a week. She felt justified in her love and showed no shame. The jury, however, already moved by Yvonne's plight, only seemed to be further swayed by Jeanette's haughty presence and testimony. In less than forty-five minutes, the jury returned with a verdict of "not guilty." And, as *Time* magazine reported, thousands of young housewives, who chose to ignore the day's rain to wait outside the courthouse, erupted in cheer. Their husbands, however, seemed a little more susceptible to the cold shiver that a cool rain could bring.

Now, of course, it's only extreme acts of passion, such as assaults and murders, that we notice; but how often have smaller decisions, such as the purchase of a fancy new car when jilted by a lover or the desire to work for a competitor when fired, been made under this same emotional influence? If our decisions were made in a calm or logical manner, would we still do what we do? When emotions are involved, it seems people are more likely to act impulsively; for good or bad.

I MUST HAVE BEEN OUT OF MY MIND

As seen with Yvonne, the desire for balance in our lives is simply a part of human nature and will often invite action. Many, in their efforts to get even or to be "fair," will seek to share their sense of loss or benefit. Some will even sacrifice their own futures or forgo their own benefits for the self desire of evenness. One good deed deserves another; an eye for an eye. No two expressions could be truer. No two desires have resulted in a poorer night's sleep or been more relevant in an emotionally enthused payback.

How many times have you heard or thought, "I'm gonna get even, if it's the last thing I do"? How many times have you reacted with emotion? People, it seems, will often look to balance their actions, and the actions of others. "I must have been out of my mind!" How many times have you said that? What was it that you did? What influenced your decision? Even to ourselves, and after the fact, we sometimes cannot fathom the things we do. But are we really at fault? Or, as even a jury might agree, are we just helplessly blinded by the overwhelming guidance our feelings will sometimes compel?

THE NEED FOR BALANCE

The tendency of our emotions to swing like a pendulum and the need for balance go hand in hand. Because we must maintain a state of balance, emotions have to be brought under control. This is often achieved by taking action.

Sir Isaac Newton was an English physicist, mathematician, astronomer, and philosopher. Born in 1643, his work in gravitation, optics, calculus, and mechanics is the foundation for modern physics. He is one of the most influential people of all time.

Although he is generally best known for his mathematical principles and research into the laws of physics, Newton wrote on religion and philosophy as well, which may make sense when you look at his three laws of motion.

According to Wikipedia, they go something like this:

First law: Every body remains at rest unless it is acted upon by an outside force.

Second law: The change in momentum of a body is proportional to the force applied to it and happens along the same line on which that force is applied.

Third law: To every action, there is always an equal and opposite reaction. Meaning that when one body exerts force on another, the forces are equal in magnitude and opposite in direction.

And now, I quote Mr. Wikipedia exactly. This law is sometimes referred to as the "action-reaction law."

Okay, I'm not saying that every emotion mandates a response, but that does frequently seem to be the case, in human nature as well as in physics.

There have been several studies investigating this same line of thinking in people. One such study was by Ernst Fehr, director of the Institute for Empirical Research of Economics at the University of Zurich in Switzerland. *BusinessWeek*, *National Geographic*, the huffingtonpost.com, and *Scientific American* were just some of the reputable sources that reviewed his findings. My favorite account however was written by Amanda Gardner, a *HealthDay* news reporter, and was featured on healingwell.com. Her article begins like this: "A Swiss brain imaging study shows that punishing people when they behave unfairly activates the same reward circuitry of the brain that is fired up when sniffing cocaine or seeing a beautiful face."

It's a pretty exciting study, so let's take a look. Its research explores the phenomenon of seeking revenge. As Ms. Gardner's article explains, the study does, in fact, suggest that we gain a sense of satisfaction when acting on emotionally driven responses, such as the doling out of punishment to others for bad behavior.

In the study, a group participated in a game where revenge could take place. The scientists measured the brain activity of the participants using a technology called positron-emission tomography, or PET. In the game, participants exchanged money back and forth. If a player made a selfish move instead of one that benefited everyone, the other players could penalize that player.

The study went pretty much like this: Certain participants were each given a sum of money. Person A could either keep his money or give some to person B. Person B would then receive an additional sum and could now reciprocate by giving some back to A. If B, however, acted selfishly, and chose not to reciprocate, A could decide to punish B.

The results showed that the majority of the players elected to impose a penalty, even when it cost some of their own money. Specifically, all fourteen players chose retaliation when the selfishness was deliberate and didn't cost them any of their own money; twelve of the fourteen players chose punishment, even if it took from their own money.

According to the PET images, the player's retaliations activated a region of the brain called the *dorsal striatum*, the area of the brain involved in enjoyment and satisfaction. The stronger the activity within this region, the stronger the punishment the participant was likely to give. So yes, it would seem that the enjoyment of revenge was indeed sweeter than the pain of loss.

Brian Knutson, professor of psychology and neuroscience at Stanford University, also reviewed the research. He stated that while he wished the experiment had included a wider variety of participants, he believes it to be important to note how emotion can interact with an analytical decision process. Professor Knutson further indicated that economists should perhaps pay more attention to people's feelings, especially before an event. He then, I think, summed it up best by stating, "Emotions are not just reactive; they can be proactive. They can actually focus and drive behavior."

THE TICKING BOM

Face-first on the ground, he could barely see the cracks in the street. It's a scene that has probably been repeated many times before. But this time, there was an audience. On the fifteenth of December in 1987, Rodney King was pulled over and forced to the ground beside his car. As a home video would document, for one minute and nineteen seconds, Mr. King would endure a continuous rain of blows. The police that were beating him never seemed to stop. From watching the repeated airings of the video on the news, one could almost believe they couldn't. They continued to rain blow after blow until it seemed they just got tired. Some said they weren't thinking; they were just reacting emotionally. They were driven by the need for retribution, the need to find balance, to feel even, as payment for King's running or failing to respond to their initial commands.

With the video's repeated showing, a firestorm of anger engulfed viewers and protests ensued. As a result of the video, four officers were charged. The subsequent lack of accountability in the upcoming verdict, however, would ignite one of the most memorable riots of our time.

On April 29, 1992, when the verdict was released, six days of rioting started that would eventually result in the deaths of fifty-three people, the injuries of two thousand others, and almost a billion dollars worth of property damage. Widespread looting, arson, assault, and murder would run rampant in the city. Over 3,500 fires would destroy 1,100 buildings.

The rioters, to say the least, were emotionally charged; and, as with most spontaneous actions of this nature, they were a group positioned to react. You see, while the verdict was the catalyst, the underlying issues within the city's core were the cause.

A special committee of the California Legislature found that poverty, segregation, lack of educational and employment opportunities, widespread perception of police abuse, and unequal consumer services were responsible. The rioters were bombs waiting to explode. The natural reaction to a consistent pattern of denial or indifference, whether real or perceived, will always take the path guided by the laws of human nature. The rioters were frustrated. They were emotionally charged.

SO WHERE ARE THE BRAKES?

The person who wants to "sleep on a decision" or states, "Well, okay, let me think about it," does so because of a previous time when he or she regretted making a decision without due consideration. It seems that some people are better at controlling their emotions when making decisions.

And others, who may not be good at resisting temptation, will at least recognize their "sway susceptibility" and keep themselves out of certain situations. They understand their own impulsiveness, and will often go to great lengths to ensure their limited ability to act. They will coach themselves to stay away from temptations, like a compulsive gambler will try to avoid a casino or an alcoholic will try to avoid an evening at a nightclub.

Additionally, some people are able to weigh their need for balance against the costs that they themselves may incur. So yes, it seems that not everyone responds to every emotion in the same way or to the same degree.

But the only real point here is that sometimes an influencer will have to hit a moving target. Because everyone, and I mean everyone, except the extreme physicist who designs bridges or examines the metallurgical makeup of various objects for the study of heat dissipation, has a hot button. Sometimes it just takes the skilled to find it.

The officers who pulled Rodney King over felt they didn't get the respect they deserved. The LA rioters felt they didn't get the same level of consideration and support as others in their community. Yvonne Chevallier loved her husband, and he gave her less in return.

WE'RE ONLY HUMAN

Dr. Jennifer Lerner, a professor at the Harvard Kennedy School and director of the Harvard Laboratory for Decision Science, is one of the leading researchers in the field of human decision making. In many of her studies, she has successfully documented the relationship between emotion and the decision making process. In one such study, Dr. Lerner examined the relationship between a person's emotional state and his or her willingness to spend.

For the study, she gathered a group of participants to watch a selected film. One group was shown a sad film, a clip of *The Champ*, which portrays a boy experiencing the pain and helplessness of watching his mentor decline. Another group was selected to watch an emotionally neutral film, one about the Great Barrier Reef. Each film was about four minutes long. After watching the different clips, each group was asked a series of questions that were presented as random. But in reality, the questions were selected to determine how their varying emotional states might affect certain buying situations. Dr. Lerner's findings showed that participants who watched the sad film were willing to pay up to 300% more for a particular item than those who watched the neutral film. She suggests that the emotion of sadness triggers the desire to change one's circumstances, thus the participants' willingness to pay increased prices. Even if the sadness is derived from a previous and unrelated event, it rouses a need to make a change. Thus sad or tragic events will likely encourage buying sprees rather than discourage them. Sadness, it seems, makes us devalue ourselves. The propensity to pay more may be an attempt to elevate our own worth.

In other studies, Dr. Lerner examined the emotions of anger and disgust. She found that disgust will trigger the desire to expel, thus likely reducing buying and selling prices. Anger will further compel us to demand a lower price, which in turn strengthens our ability to negotiate. So, this offers both the influencer and the influencee a lesson: Creating and timing an emotional swing can and may ultimately sway someone to an influencer's direction of choice. It also makes sense not to anger an influencee, or to at least wait until the influencee's anger has faded before seeking an agreement.

FREE AT LAST

On a cool day in December of 2010, rapper G. Dep walked into a New York City police station and said,

"Seventeen years ago, I shot someone." After verifying the facts, the officers on duty were able to begin the process of closing a case that had been cold for seventeen years. Apparently haunted by his secret, Mr. Dep could take it no more.

G. Dep was born Trevell Coleman. He grew up on the tough streets of New York. In the early hours of October 19, 1993, he was robbing a man named John Henkel outside an East Harlem apartment complex. When Henkel tried to resist, Dep shot him three times in the chest with a .40-caliber handgun, killing him.

Almost twenty years later, with very little possibility of ever being caught, Dep came forward. He said the attack had eaten at him for years. After his confession, he confided to the *New York Post*, "I wonder if all the bad things that happened to me in my life were karma for what I did . . ." He further stated, "I thought if I turned myself in, it might give me closure."

G. Dep was in the middle of a comeback when he confessed; his album *Ghetto Legend* was soon to be released on the Internet. He had also been quite successful when he was younger. His 2001 debut album was called *Child of the Ghetto*. He was one of the rising stars on the talented and ever-driven Sean "Diddy" Combs's Bad Boy record label. His popular hit "Let's Get It" featured Diddy and Black Rob.

So. G. Dep was tough. He fought the unforgiving city streets of Harlem and survived the ups and downs of an equally brutal world of entertainment; yet even G. Dep, straight up as tough as you get, was still no match for the power of his own emotional influence. He told his lawyer, Michael Alperstein, that guided by a substance abuse program "he was trying to make amends."

IS IT HOT IN HERE?

Many will be strong. Many will fight the impact an emotion may bring. And, as we earlier stated, when having the time to coach or avoid a future decision, some will be quite effective in denying their impulse.

But what if we just happen upon a situation that invokes emotion? Or, what if we overestimate our own ability to think in a "level headed" way and put ourselves in over our heads? Can we then still control our emotions? I mean, it is all just in our heads, right?

Well, some studies indicate it's not.

Picture yourself driving over the Canadian border. Picture the warm, inviting smile of the guard as he acknowledges your greeting. Picture the majestic hills off to your left and the serene lakes that lie at their bases. You can almost taste the freshly grilled large mouth bass that will soon be smoking up the front of your cabin. No work, no phone, just a week of rest and peaceful relaxation. Ahhh. Pure peace. Finally.

Now picture the same scene at the border with four kilos of cocaine wrapped in a tight bundle hiding at the bottom of your trunk. Will you be able to move when the guard asks you to open it up? Will your desire to camouflage your fear translate to a calm response?

Walking along a curb is not really hard to do. It's plenty wide enough. If someone were to give you a hundred bucks to walk a length of it, could you do it? Sure. Why not? Now, would it be as easy if it were 475 feet in the air? Well, look down. Okay, quickly now, before you hit the ground, tell me, what was it that took your balance? Did your emotional fear encourage a physical reaction?

Look. Everybody would like to be a better poker player. Everyone wants to sit at that final table; all that cash, the bracelet, the celebrity . . . but very few ever will. This is something a true person of influence will understand. Like it or not, willing or not, emotions dictate our responses. Our internal thoughts will often, consciously or not, push us off the curb, or even tell on us.

THE BIG BROWN EYES OF KATY

Sure, the crumbling wall of the poorly constructed block home, the worn and discolored blanket held tightly in her arms, and the rock covered dirt field that doubles as her front yard all add to the picture; but they are not the deciding factors. When deciding whether to contribute to the charity's cause or not, it's the big brown eyes of little Katy that may just influence a decision.

Have you ever dug a little deeper when moved by a certain situation? Picture the amount of your donation with and without the graphics. The scene captures you, arouses your empathy; Katy's presence makes it personal, attaches "realness" that encourages you to react. Emotions and their known reactions are guiding factors behind any marketing strategy. A touching image is a powerful trigger. If you feel compassion from viewing the image, if you "suffer" with little Katy, you will feel compelled to help her. Compassion, anger, fear, and even determined avoidance are evoked when confronted with scenes designed to bring them out. And presto, once the viewer feels the desired emotion, the desired reaction kicks in.

THE EMOTIONAL SWING

Stories and research are meant to encourage interest and awareness. They can also help create a bridge for applying new information to one's own life. Please recognize the relevance of this. Whether you are the influencer or the influencee, a salesperson or a customer, insight and understanding are the seeds for future success. A better understanding of emotions and their influences will better enable you to make and seek desired choices.

While I was growing up, there is no doubt in my mind that many of my decisions and actions were the result of my emotions at the time. But it wasn't until after I had been working in sales for a while that I started to recognize the true extent of this power. It seemed that in every step of a sale, from a customer's initial interest to their final decision, emotions dictated their path. A person was always more likely to enact a decision when his or her emotions were somehow involved. And this can be more than just a focused intention, such as using fear to help sell a security alarm or sympathy to fund a cause. When people are in a heightened state of emotion, any emotion, an influencer can more easily influence a direction by simply indicating a path.

One of the more interesting examples of this influence can be witnessed during the height of the sale, meaning while the final terms are being discussed. It is here, that sometimes a strangely misplaced anger can be inexplicably aroused in a customer. This can happen because a sales environment typically causes apprehension, and when getting down to the final details, this apprehension can morph into frustration and even anger. Some believe it is the intent or fault of the staff to cause this frustration, and will take and show their offense.

However, a customer's anger can actually, more often than not, work in favor of making a sale. I know, but hold on. You see emotions swing. The more explosive an individual's reaction, the more likely they are to buy. As we talked about earlier, this happens because of the need for an emotional balance. A person will rarely maintain a state of anger in situations that are time sensitive. Once a person's emotions explode, the person's natural reaction is to try and make up for it, to swing back to a more balanced state. When customers show their anger, they then often feel "bad" and seek to make up for it by being more open and accepting. So, when a salesperson offers to make peace, customers will often jump at the chance. And in an effort to achieve a state of balance, they will often swing past the point of equilibrium, which swings them toward favoring the salesperson. Customers are often more agreeable after showing their anger than they were initially. This is basically the principle behind make up sex. The emotion of the preceding argument creates a passionate desire to both act and make amends.

WAS THAT ME?

Do you remember when an assistant coach for the New York Jets was suspended for tripping a player during a football game? He admitted he did it. He apologized, saying, "It showed a total lapse in judgment." But, was it really his fault? Well, let's take a look.

In December of 2010, Nolan Carroll, a rookie for the Miami Dolphins, stumbled, lost his footing, and crashed to the ground while running toward the opposing teams punt returner. Cool. There was now one less potential tackler in the Dolphins' attempt to clear the field. But wait a minute. Replay the event.

If you watch the video, you will see Mr. Carroll was running up the sideline toward the field of play. In fact he was so close to the line that the Jets' assistant barely had to move to trip him. A mere quiver could have done the job. Now, I ask you, was this something the assistant coach planned or wanted to do?

While one side of the assistant coach's brain knew the cameras were rolling and that it was wrong to trip Carroll, the other side was passionately rooting for his team and only wanted to help. It's hard to tell exactly, but it appears his intent was just to stand close to the line, to discourage a full use of the field.

But, as Carroll got closer, something happened. The assistant coach's mind was willing his team to win so badly that his brain triggered a slight physical reaction that the other side of his brain, the side of reason, was unable to stop. The result, he tripped Carroll. He probably wasn't even aware he'd moved until Carroll fell, but by then, it was too late.

You see, the body is filled with millions of nerves, all waiting to be fired when told. These nerves, I believe, are no different than the ones that cause us to sweat when we are nervous or turn red when we are mad. They are uncontrollable reactions that are triggered by uncontrollable emotions. Sometimes our bodies just act automatically.

Have you ever noticed that the doctor stands to the side when he or she wants to test your reflexes with the little rubber hammer? That's because the doctor understands how we work. Even when we focus, prepare, and are 100 percent aware of our environment and intention, it may not matter; our emotions will takeover.

I think one of the best examples of this is the consistent accuracy the standard lie detector will exhibit. Although many will try, it is just about impossible to beat. Even with specific mind control exercises and training, it cannot be beat with any certainty. Why? Well I think you already know. Emotions don't lie.

CONCLUSION

Emotions drive us. They can sway us toward surprising actions and behaviors, like confessing to twenty-year-old crimes, getting in someone's way, killing an unfaithful lover, giving money to charity, buying a car, or anything else. Those who want to influence others should always be aware of what others are feeling, because emotions are powerful influencers that can change from moment to moment.

When our emotions swing, we can go from feeling pity to feeling anger in a second. We can go from planning to shoot ourselves to putting a bullet in the chest of the one we love. A person's emotional swing can never be discounted. In these examples, we can also see that emotional influence doesn't end after a person's initial reaction. By recognizing and adapting to the new emotions we see, we can influence people to make new decisions. New actions will always bring on new emotions, and subsequently, new decisions will be made. Until the final decision is settled, the possibility of new influence is always present.

MOMENTUM

Ever wonder how much a tech company makes on its "game box" compared to how much it makes on its games? Or why the cell phones we're walking around with were likely free? In the courts, in business, and in life, momentum is often the result of a commitment, and this is a powerful influence.

A first date, a finished basement, the pepperoni on your pizza, an extended warranty, credit card miles, and even the stamp on your sandwich card all have a higher purpose. Because commitment encourages momentum, an influencer can benefit by making it happen. Human nature has certain biases, and these will likely lead us to a path of acceptance. Once a person commits, they are more likely to follow through. A customer, a recruit and a lover are all more likely to make concessions or extend their flexibility to keep an initial arrangement intact. They will more likely agree to demands that they would initially have been unlikely to make, just to stay the course.

Earlier we mentioned the three laws of motion in physics and how they apply to our emotions. Well, another law of physics is that it takes much less energy to maintain an object's direction than it does to change it. That is the principle that applies here.

PROOF WITH A REASONABLE DOUBT

On January 4, 2011, a Texas judge declared Cornelius Dupree an innocent man. After spending the majority of his life behind bars, he could now finally spend time with the family he was unable to be a part of for most of his adult life. Since his conviction for aggravated robbery with a deadly weapon on April 3, 1980, Mr. Dupree had, for thirty years, declared his innocence.

It all started back in 1979 when a young female, twenty six years old at the time, and her male friend were approached by two men in the parking lot of a small grocery store. The two men forced the girl and her friend into their car at gunpoint. Once in transit, the men robbed the two, taking their money and valuables. The perpetrators then forced the male to pull over and ordered him out of the car. Then they continued to a nearby park and raped the girl.

Barely a week later, Mr. Dupree, only nineteen at the time, and a friend, Anthony Massengill, were stopped while on their way to a party, approximately two miles from the grocery parking lot where the crime had occurred. They fit a description. The following day, the female victim selected Dupree's photograph from an array of photos. The male victim, however, was unable to select either defendant from the same photo array. But at the trial four months later, both victims identified Dupree and Massengill as their attackers, though the female victim repeatedly misidentified a photo of Massengill for Dupree, before finally getting it "right." The victims were both white; Dupree and Massengill were both black.

According to the Innocence Project, a nonprofit organization, 265 people have been exonerated by DNA evidence between 1989, the first year DNA became valid, and 2010.

The average time served by each individual within this period was just over thirteen years, amounting to almost 3,500 years of life in a cell that shouldn't have been served. Seventeen of those individuals had the pleasure of serving their times on death row. Even more incredible, during the same period, there were tens of thousands of cases where prime suspects were identified and pursued, only to be proven innocent by DNA testing.

Barry Scheck, a director with the Innocence Project, summed Dupree's case up the only way one could: "Cornelius Dupree spent the prime of his life behind bars because of mistaken identification that probably wouldn't have happened if the best practices now used in Dallas had been deployed." He then said that in many areas these "best practices" are still not being used.

So, what do you say to a man who just spent thirty years in a cage for a crime he didn't commit? Really. I don't know. What do you say?

It makes a person wonder, what if this were to happen to me? Or, how many other innocent people are still in jail because the evidence to free them hasn't yet been processed? Worse yet, how many will never be cleared because there is no evidence to free them?

Daniel S. Medwed, a professor of law at the University of Utah and a staunch advocate in the pursuit of justice for the innocent, has extensively researched how the innocent are found guilty. Professor Medwed has postulated that the people involved in the process of protecting are simply following certain human behaviors that will often mislead them. The police that investigate the crimes, the eyewitnesses who identify the suspects, and the prosecutors who try the cases may all suffer from a series of human cognitive biases, meaning that they will all feel that the initial suspect is the one who is more likely to be guilty simply because he was originally thought to be guilty. This belief often begins with the police who make the arrest.

In the early stages of an investigation, a phenomenon called "tunnel vision" can occur. This happens when an officer subconsciously commits to believing that the first suspect is guilty, so the officer strictly focuses on that suspect. The momentum created from this early commitment often sets the stage for the outcome of a trial. Initial bias on the part of the police commits them to a course of action that may actually deter them from rationally reviewing additional evidence.

According to University of Wisconsin professors Michael Scott and Keith Findley, police tunnel vision occurs when detectives overestimate the evidence against a particular suspect and subconsciously disregard the possibility of alternate perpetrators or exculpatory evidence. The professors explain that the foundation for tunnel vision in the criminal investigative system lies in "expectation" or "confirmation bias." When someone starts something, that person is often inclined to see it through.

Alafair Burke, a professor of law at Hofstra University and an acclaimed author, sees it the same way. She proposes that after the detectives develop a theory about someone or something, this bias may encourage them to selectively process newfound information in a manner that confirms rather than challenges their original theory. Even when confronted with information that contradicts their original theory, they may still cling to it.

In her awakening article "Improving Prosecutorial Decision Making: Some Lessons of Cognitive Science," Professor Burke explains how such an influence can occur. In her article, she breaks down four factors of influence that contribute to imperfect decision making. They are confirmation bias, selective information processing, belief perseverance, and the avoidance of cognitive dissonance, all profound factors of influence.

Confirmation bias is the likeliness that people will look to support rather than question any theories under review. Using empirical research, research that is based on experimentation or observation, researchers have shown that people will naturally prefer to favor evidence that follows their initial belief. This even appears to be the case when the evidence involved is questioned to determine its validity. As a supporting example, Professor Burke offered the study of Mark Snyder and William Swann, who are well known for their study "Hypothesis Testing Processes in Social Interaction." In their study, subjects were told to "test" whether people were "introverts" or "extroverts" with a series of questions. The results convincingly showed that the subjects were more likely to only ask the questions that would prove their working hypotheses and not those that would disprove them. For example, the results indicate that when a person forms an early impression of a new acquaintance, they may wish to test their hypotheses based only upon their expectations.

Selective information processing suggests that people are less likely to objectively evaluate evidence independently from their prior belief. Meaning they overvalue the findings that are consistent with their theory and undervalue information that is inconsistent. As a result, a detective or prosecutor may base his or her belief of guilt on potentially flawed information, like the information from a current inmate seeking a deal, a subconsciously guided misidentification of a suspect, or a coerced confession.

Belief perseverance is where a person will stick to his or her theory even when contradictory evidence indicates otherwise. As Professor Burke eloquently states, belief perseverance is where human cognition departs from rational decision making not through the biased assimilation of ambiguous information, but by failing to adjust a theory in response to proof that prior information is demonstrably false. It is where a person will blindly stick to his or her early commitment.

The avoidance of cognitive dissonance is where a person will prefer to have his or her outward actions align with an inner belief. Meaning it is much easier to carry out something when you believe in it and often difficult when you do not. For example, a salesman who believes in his product or service is more likely, on a performance basis, to succeed than one who does not. Research has shown that performing an act or carrying out a request that a person disagrees with will actually cause the person discomfort, making the person's approach stilted.

This appears to be quite prevalent in the feelings of many.

Once the officer is "satisfied," the case goes to the prosecutor. And while this is where legal experts agree an unworthy case should end, this is often where a further commitment is made.

The criminal court system is based upon the premise that you must be guilty beyond a reasonable doubt. However, the potential problems for an accurate verdict in the cases without physical evidence are replete with the possibility of error. Too often an ill advised influence will be present throughout the process. And, once the process starts, it can snowball. With the initial suspicion of guilt, the commitment to keep that guilt is followed and then passed on: an officer believes in a suspect's guilt, a witness wants to believe in a suspect's guilt, the prosecutor trusts in the officer's belief, and the jury trusts in the prosecutor's belief.

In each circumstance, a degree of influence will always be present. A witness won't want to disappoint the victim or the police, so he or she may unconsciously make an error in their claim. Even if a hint or suggestive implication helps a witness to identify a suspect, whether intentionally or unconsciously, what may occur may occur. The case will then proceed to the prosecutor, who will often simply follow the lead of the police. It is here that prosecutors will unlikely disagree with or question the investigating officers, because they work with them most every day and won't want to break their bond. The prosecutors also realize that they may need the officers' compliance sometime down the road. And now, for the final "dismissal" in what should be a dismissal, the prosecutor can further justify a willingness to charge by feeling that he or she is leaving it "in the hands of the jury." And, of course, the jury will often follow the prosecutor's lead. Many people, believe it or not, will start and often continue to feel, "Well, the suspect must be guilty, or the suspect wouldn't have been arrested." And so the cycle continues.

OKAY, I DID IT

Many of the innocent who were released, or had their charges dismissed, had actually confessed. And you're probably thinking that if they confessed, they must be guilty. However, this is not necessarily true. Irrefutable DNA evidence, bolstered sometimes by the finding of the real perpetrator, has shown that innocent people will in fact confess. Hard to believe, I know, but let me explain.

In addition to the influencing biases and pressures that an officer will face, there are also other factors that may further an officer's intent. In the research of Findley and Scott, they explain that an officer is often judged by his or her "clearance rate," meaning the actual number of cases an officer closes. As a result, officers are even further pressured or influenced to complete their cases. For some, this will up the ante in closing their investigations. Additionally, some may simply believe that it doesn't really matter how they get a confession; if someone eventually admits, then that person must be guilty. Kind of like the end justifies the means. Or they may just not realize how well they are at persuading, or how weak an innocent suspect may be.

So, in their desire to complete a case and gain a confession, they will naturally look to increase the likeliness of getting a confession. One way, detectives have found, that works quite well is to exaggerate the evidence they have and its likely punishment for the suspect during "questioning." Then explain that the suspect's best hope for help or leniency is to "admit" now. The detectives will sometimes also threaten to influence the prosecutor and judge into seeking the harshest penalty possible if the suspect does not cooperate. You have to admit, this type of persuasion is quite intimidating and is also quite effective. As you know, some are more susceptible to influence than others.

Professors Scott and Findley's research shows us that most officers are trained with what is called the "Reid Technique" of interrogation. The manual that teaches this technique is credited to Inbau, Reid, Buckley, and Jayne, and is titled *Criminal Interrogations and Confessions*. With this technique, there are two approaches an officer will take when talking to a witness. One is an interview, where the officer's focus is centered on research and finding out certain facts. The other is an interrogation, where the officer's goal is to get a confession. In the interrogation process, there are nine separate parts, all designed to wear a suspect down and gain his or her compliance. As I explained in chapter two, "Persuasion," a designed and focused process always seems to be the best way to create the path of one's influence.

Once a police officer commits to the interrogation process, the officer will follow the process to break the suspect by convincing the suspect that he or she is doomed, thus making the suspect think that confessing is the rational or risk-reducing choice. The first steps in the interrogation process are designed to overcome resistance. This is done by isolating the suspect and then confronting him or her with assertions of guilt. Officers want the suspect to believe that the police know the individual is guilty and that the police have the evidence to prove it. It is during this stage of the process that the interrogator will often confront the suspect with false evidence of his or her guilt, such as an eyewitness to the crime or a surveillance video. The officers are then trained to alternate their behaviors between aggression and understanding to emotionally involve the suspect in an attempt to reason that the suspect's best option is to confess. So the police are subconsciously committing even more to their own initial belief. With this procedure, cognitive biases are openly encouraged. Additionally, because the police are also trained to read a suspect's behavior, the police will follow what they read off a suspect, potentially increasing their efforts in gaining a confession.

Now, you and I, and the professors who have studied this are all most likely realists. This method of persuasion can, and often does, lead to true confessions. In many cases, certain additional verifiable facts are disclosed.

But where there is use, there is also the possibility of error, and when no additional proof is offered to support a coerced confession from an innocent person, some type of flag needs to be raised. If no additional information comes to light or a suspect's decree contradicts other evidence in some way, someone needs to step up. There needs to be more responsibility and more accountability at the point of filing the charges. There are secondary overseers in many districts, but there needs to be one in all of them. In the opinion of many, this should especially be the case where the poor or underprivileged reside, because this is most likely where a miscarriage of justice will occur. There is often more indifference or abuse where people don't have the economical or outside support to encourage a more responsible look.

Okay, by now you might see some additional pressure to confess and even recognize its possible effect. But are you convinced? Are you? Or do you still believe that you, and most others, should simply withstand the pressure and just say no?

Well, that might not be your best option. Let's try another approach, but this time I want you to put yourself in the arrestee's position at the end, and then ask yourself what you would do.

Another reason that people will falsely confess, even in court, is because they are forced to choose between the lesser of two evils. Let me explain.

To increase the chances of gaining a confession or of keeping a high clearance rate, an arresting officer will often look to charge a suspect with multiple offenses. Because doing so will raise the odds that at least one charge will "stick." This practice has become quite common, even acceptable. And it is typically enacted at the outset, when the officers form an initial belief, to further make a suspect seem guilty. In fact, police officers will often look for as many complementary charges as they can. Some of which, if you've ever read a charging document, are quite duplicitous. So the main reason an innocent person will "confess" or plead guilty is because the police realize that charging an individual with multiple offenses gives them leverage, leverage to coax a suspect into agreeing to a lesser charge in a possible plea deal, whether the suspect is guilty or not.

You see, the police understand that most cases will never see a trial. The system is so busy that the majority of the time an early resolution is often encouraged. With the leverage of multiple charges, the police are in a better position to sway for a plea. For the accused, it is no longer about being guilty or innocent, and the accused knows this. It is about whether a jury will or will not find the accused guilty. Although the common person or potential juror may not know this, the practice is quite common. Perhaps the police subconsciously justify adding additional charges to a suspect's arrest because their initial belief, the one that says the arrestee is guilty of the first charge, influences them to create more leverage against the accused. Perhaps another reason is that the police will sometimes allow their frustrations with the system or the perceived "red tape" involved in keeping a person's civil liberties intact to get the better of them.

A potential source for an officer's additional bias is also possibly influenced by looking at their arrestee's previous record. Even if only subconsciously, an officer will recognize that a previous charge is also more likely to be believed as a future charge. This can also be a factor in their initial bias. If an arrestee has a past arrest or conviction, the natural inclination for the belief of recurrence or a pattern of continuation is again simply human nature. The assumption process of being seen as a repeat offender is of course not limited to any one group of people. The police understand the jury will likely agree as well.

Like it or not, despite the fact that the vast majority of our officers are inherently good, overworked, underpaid, and underappreciated, they can still make early commitments based on biases that can then influence others, causing the momentum to put an innocent person in jail.

So, back to my question: If you were wrongly accused of something and circumstantial evidence, such as a misidentification or a misguided theory, pointed blame in your direction, would you admit to a lesser charge to avoid the risk of a bigger charge? Would you, without question, trust the judgment of twelve jurors, twelve strangers, with your future? Would you gamble that your attorney was more persuasive than the attorney of the state?

What if you were poor and could only afford a public defender? What if you were black in a mostly white county? What if you were not as educated or as experienced as the other people involved? What if you had a past record, would that influence your decision? Do you think it would influence the decision of the jury?

So, last time. Don't answer out loud, just to yourself. If circumstance put you in the wrong place at the wrong time and the momentum created by the arresting officers' biases carried you to this decision, would you confess to a lesser charge, something you hadn't done, to avoid a bigger one?

Scary, isn't it?

ALPHABETICAL LIST OF SOME BIASES WE FACE

Since commitment is so integral to creating momentum, I think it's reasonable to take a quick look at some of the common biases that may influence our actions.

Bandwagon effect: The tendency to believe or follow because others are already doing so.

Belief perseverance: The tendency to stick to a theory even when evidence contradicts it.

Confirmation bias: The tendency to look for and interpret information in ways that confirm preconceptions.

Contrast effect: The tendency to perceive a reduction or an increase in an object's value when it's compared to a contrasting object.

Disconfirmation bias: The tendency to view evidence that contradicts one's current belief more critically or less objectively.

Endowment effect: The tendency to value something more when one takes ownership.

Illusion of control: The tendency to believe we have more control or influence over an outcome than we actually do.

Loss aversion: The tendency to prefer avoiding a loss over taking a risk that might result in a gain.

Mere exposure effect: The tendency to like what we are familiar with.

Outcome bias: The tendency to judge a decision based on its eventual outcome, rather than the worthiness of making the decision.

Selective perception: The tendency for our expectations to affect what we perceive.

Status quo bias: The tendency to resist change, and the desire for things to stay the same.

OKAY, BUT WHAT'S THE CATCH?

As you can see, the momentum garnered from an initial commitment can be quite powerful. How an innocent man can be found guilty through a process that is supposed to verify his guilt at each stage is overwhelming. But this type of influence does not just affect those in unfortunate positions.

For many businesses, their whole operating structure is based on this particular influence. Businesses rely on customers' commitments. How many times have you heard, "I've been a Ford man my whole life"? How many of you will choose the same brand of appliances that your parents had while you were growing up?

In the world of marketing, there is something called the "loss leader." It is a particular item or offering that is for sale to the public for free or at a loss. Of course, the loss leader is offered with the knowledge that the "enticement" will likely encourage customers to purchase additional items, which is where the profit will be made. So. If a large department store were to choose to lose money on its cosmetics, would that be a bad decision? Ummm, no. You see, everyone needs certain items, so certain items are bought more often and their prices are more likely to be familiar to buyers. So a buyer will recognize this particular item for comparison more than others, thus better enticing a commitment to shop there and further creating an opportunity for nearby items to be purchased while shopping. Just curious, ever been offered a free sample?

For you, as a person who reads, this might seem obvious. Or if you're a sales manager, who regularly witnesses how relevant a commitment is in gaining a sale, it probably is as well. However, this is still an influence that is sparingly used in many individuals personal life for gain. So, this can actually make a quite effective influence when encouraging a personal decision in the favor of your desire. Gain a commitment and you will better influence your collective future.

Maybe some people choose not to benefit from the influence momentum can garner because they may feel it's "wrong." It just doesn't feel right to them. Others may choose not to use it because they feel they may scare the other person away with the early commitment needed to start the process.

But to be truly effective in the art of influence, you are going to have to let these thoughts fall to the side. The key is to gain the little commitments that will lead to the bigger commitment down the road. Start small, so it is easier for someone to agree or find acceptance with the terms you're offering. Then build on the person's initial commitment with additional commitments as you go along.

Take car sales. The first step in any negotiation is to gain a commitment to purchase. Without a commitment to purchase, you have no place to go. If you negotiate a "sale price" without a commitment, all you're doing is giving the customer a number in which to shop around with. But with a commitment, even if it is contingent on agreeing to the final terms, a person is much more likely to make the purchase. Once someone agrees to buy on some premise, that person is much more likely to follow through. Again, the biases that our natures follow will always provide us with the best path to acceptance. Even if a customer had to make certain concessions during the negotiation process that the individual would not have initially accepted, the customer's earlier commitment will still move the customer toward a sale.

THE AUCTION

No one understands the power of this factor better than the auctioneer. He is the king of momentum and commitment. Even on a cold, windy day at Manheim, the world's largest auto auction, nobody can bring the heat like their professional auctioneers. They know how and where to light the fire to gain a commitment that will build into an inferno. Instinctively reading the intentions of bidders and using fast, repetitive speech, the auctioneers use the law of momentum to carry bidders past their limits to the sellers' goals. And all the auctioneer needs is a bidder's initial commitment.

Even online auctions, operating without the benefit of a personal influencer, rely on the same principle. The reason that opening bids for most items are so low is to attract interest and encourage participation. This gets people to make that first commitment. This commitment creates an emotional attachment that is driven by a competitiveness to win or by a desire for a greater feeling of self worth. And this, coupled with the influence of emotion, will often create the desire to win.

FIRST AND GOAL ON THE SEVEN

Sometimes commitment occurs by design, and sometimes it's the byproduct of circumstance. But in either situation, it is quite often the event that turns the tide.

Have you ever watched a game and seen how, for a while, everything goes one team's way; the momentum of play becomes a force in itself? This power, it often seems, is further influenced by the positive attitude of the winning team and the negative attitude of the losing team.

In order to break this momentum, the opposing team has to find or create the commitment needed to turn the tide. They have to stop, "call a time-out," and refocus. They have to resist their own negativity, slow the momentum of the opposing team, and break the trend with a play or event that lights their own fire.

The impact of this influence has been shown at recent Super Bowls and other games of importance. The grandness of the event often increases the effect. Momentum is always heightened by the electric nature of a circumstance. However, with one interception, a new momentum can change everything.

PAIR OF ACES

With two jacks in his hand and a third on the flop, the poker player knows an all in move may scare away any future bets. This is why, like in my earlier example, the auctioneer starts low and the bidder may hesitate to enter the fray. The three know that they may get caught up in the momentum.

But if the player can raise the stakes by checking or placing a small bet, he may be able to encourage, or at least not scare away, a potential bettor. Then, once fellow players are involved, it is more likely they will follow their investments. With slow play, it is human nature to keep playing the hand, as the pressure of the money already invested weighs heavily in the balance. Though a player might ordinarily fold the hand, because of the likeliness of losing, his money is already in so he is committed. His opponent, by keeping the bet low, has used the power of momentum.

WELL, I'M HERE NOW

One day, while working in sales, a woman arrived at the showroom where I was working. She had traveled a long distance and was excited to see the item she had come to buy. But unknown to the salesperson who had encouraged her trip, the item in question had incurred some damage between the time of their conversation and the time of her visit. While retrieving the item, the salesperson was confronted with this quite visible damage. He was devastated. On the way back to the showroom, he planned how he could apologize for wasting this woman's time. He genuinely felt bad, but it was obvious to him that he would have to explain what occurred and hope that she wouldn't be too upset for having made such a long trip for nothing.

On his return, he explained what had happened and offered his sincere regret. He apologized for her trip and hoped that she wouldn't catch too much traffic as she returned home. As he walked toward the door, as if to walk the woman out, she asked him where he was going. He turned around and returned her look, puzzled at her inquiry. Without hesitation, she said, "Look, I didn't drive three hours not to buy something. Show me what you got."

TIME PRESSURE

When first bidding on a newly listed item, how calm are you? How rational is your thought process? It's just you, eBay, and plenty of time. It is now three days later, the auction is about to close, and you are still calm and rational. Because that's how you roll, cool as a cucumber. Bidding is a calm, rational, and calculated process. You set a budget and stick to your plan. Ten minutes left. It's still smooth sailing. Then: *boom*. Like a thief in the night, you never saw them coming. Now what?

When we make a decision, like it or not, time is often a factor. When time is limited, we are forced to make a decision based solely on the facts that we have at hand, namely the information in the last frame in our roll of film. Time limits our ability to analytically process a decision.

So. Will you go higher than you originally wanted? As the seconds click down, eight, seven, six, five, four, three, two . . .

Quick, what's it gonna be?

Time pressure is a powerful driving force in sales and in life. A limited supply, an expiring rebate, rising interest rates, a ticking biological clock, and even the last call for alcohol all influence people's decisions. How many tickets, accidents, babies, and imperfect purchases were the result of beating a deadline? A last second pardon, the hasty renewal of an expiring law, the watchful eye of your boss as you rush through the door, and a sloppy report are but a few of life's everyday examples of time pressure and its effects.

If you think time doesn't matter, try pulling up to McDonald's at 10:01 a.m. and ordering an Egg McMuffin. We all know what the cashier's response will be.

The impact of this influence often has a broader reach than others. It may not just force a quicker move. It could limit your ability to act in the manner that you normally would. As history has shown, time pressure often promotes both irrational and regrettable decisions.

A SECOND OPINION

On January 28, 1986, seventy three seconds after it left its launching pad at Kennedy Space Center, the space shuttle *Challenger* disintegrated, spreading thousands of pieces across the Atlantic Ocean off the coast of Florida. The twisted pieces of metal and fiber could be seen falling for miles. Silently, the crowd could only watch in horror. Despite the obvious, they continued to stare, perhaps wishing they could somehow replay what they were seeing. The explosion killed all seven crew members.

Whether at the site or over the course of its many network airings, the whole world witnessed the tragedy. Which led to one question: Why?

As it often happens in our world of "right now," NASA was facing immediate pressure as to what went wrong. As public outcry pressed for answers, the press criticized NASA for not being forthcoming in its response. In their impatience, the media speculated on the possible cause. It presented a defect in an external tank as the likely source of the problem. NASA, however, reversing their soon-to-be-discovered fault, chose to endure any outside pressure for a quick finding and carefully searched, concentrating instead on the shuttle's solid rocket boosters.

As the Presidential Commission assigned to investigate the accident would soon find, NASA was correct in its early belief. The commission, also known as the Rogers Commission, named after its chairman William P. Rogers, worked for several months and published its findings. It concluded that the accident had occurred as the result of a malfunction in the solid rocket boosters. It seemed that an O-ring failure had allowed hot gases and eventually flames to be released, compromising the adjacent external tank. The failure of the O-ring was attributed to a faulty design that was susceptible to the low temperatures present on launch day.

The solid rocket boosters, or SRBs, are a source of propellant for the shuttle during liftoff. Each SRB is constructed of six sections joined by three factory joints and three field joints. The factory joints are welded; the field joints, however, because they are assembled on-site, are sealed by a pair of rubber O-rings. One is the primary seal, and the other is the backup. The seals are supposed to contain the high-pressure gases that are produced by the burning propellant inside the booster and then forced out of the aft end of each rocket.

More encompassing in its search, the Presidential Commission would also give its findings on the additional factors that it felt contributed to the accident. It found that both NASA and Morton Thiokol, the maker of the O-rings, had failed to adequately respond to the potential risk of the flawed joint design. The commission also strongly questioned the decision making process that had led to the final approval of the launch and the factors that might have contributed to the decision. As a result of its study, the commission presented NASA's "unrealistically optimistic" launch schedule as a possible key contributing factor in the accident.

NASA's *Challenger* was originally scheduled to launch on the twenty-second of January. It was, however, delayed until January 23, because of the delays that the previous mission of the space shuttle *Columbia* suffered. The shuttle *Columbia* had landed about ten days earlier after returning from its seventh mission. The launch was then pushed back to the twenty-fourth, after further review suggested that more time was still needed. It was rescheduled again, this time for the twenty-fifth of January, because of bad weather at the landing site in Dakar, Senegal. The site was then changed to Casablanca, but that site was not equipped for night landings, so the launch date was adjusted once more to keep the planned space activities unchanged. Predictions for a chance of rain at Kennedy Space Center resulted in the rescheduling of the flight until the morning of the twenty-seventh. On the twenty-seventh, the flight was delayed again because of problems with the exterior access hatch. By the time the problems were corrected, crosswinds at the landing site were deemed unfavorable. As the team waited for conditions to settle, the launch window ran out. January 28 would be the day.

The day looked promising, at least in regard to all the previous reasons for delay. Many people were looking forward to the launch.

But the engineers at Morton Thiokol, the contractor responsible for the construction and operation of the SRBs, were concerned about the predicted temperature in the area of Kennedy. They were concerned that the unusually low temperatures would have an adverse effect on the resiliency of the O-rings responsible for sealing the SRBs. In a teleconference call on the evening of the twenty-seventh, Morton Thiokol's managers relayed their fears to NASA's managers at both Kennedy Space Center and Marshall Space Flight Center.

Marshall Space Flight Center was mission control. The engineers were worried that the seals would fail to hold if the temperature fell below fifty-three degrees Fahrenheit. They were concerned because no testing had been done below that temperature, so they didn't know if the joint could seal properly.

In their communications, they argued that the low overnight temperatures could actually fall below forty degrees Fahrenheit, the minimum threshold for safety. But this was an argument that NASA personnel dismissed because they reasoned that if one failed, the second one would provide the seal. Which by the way was a direct violation of policy. The decision to go or not should have fallen only on the ability of a primary system to perform as specified. The backup was purely that, a backup.

So, on the day of the launch, despite the concerns of their engineers, Morton Thiokol management recommended that the launch continue as scheduled.

Thiokol management was, it appeared, influenced by NASA's desire to maintain the flight schedule. In chapter eight of the Presidential Commission Report, titled "Pressures on the System," the undeniable influence of time pressure was evident. According to the report, from the beginning, NASA had planned for the *Challenger* shuttle to be a "vehicle" that would make space explorations "routine and economical." The greater number of flights, the more routine and the more economical; so an accelerated flight schedule was conceived. But the result was the dilution of human and material resources that were available for any particular flight. Thus, pressures developed from the need to meet their customer commitments. The necessity to launch a certain number of flights and launch them on time was imperative to the perceived success of the program. Such considerations, like time pressure, had the potential to obscure engineering concerns.

In the aftermath of the accident, NASA recognized the potential for such pressures and attempted to aim at more realistic flight schedules. Many changes were made. And while there will always be setbacks and influences that will sway any given action, I am confident that these changes will prevent further accidents. Because, although still human, I personally know they employ the smartest people on earth.

TIME IS MONEY

When the concrete truck comes, the rebar better be set. When the tile contractor arrives, the bathroom walls better be up and sealed.

Overtime pay, the firing of slow contractors, the bribing of inspectors, the cutting of corners, and unfortunate mistakes are all often secondary to the deadline.

With quotas to fill, one has to wonder, what percentage of business is conducted at the end of the month? Is a person really any more or less able to sell or buy based on another person's need to meet his or her end-of-the-month projections? And, more importantly, how will this outside pressure affect the quality of your decisions?

Like how a seasoned pilot may justify an ill-advised takeoff and kill hundreds of people to keep his schedule, or how you accept the red car that's in stock instead of the blue one you really want to avoid missing out on an expiring rebate, it seems that we are all sometimes at the mercy of our own pressure.

FIRST COME, FIRST SERVE

It was beautiful. Mille Miglia Red. And like the name implies, I could see it from a thousand miles away. For six months, I cut, split, and delivered firewood in my dad's truck, just waiting for this day. I was beyond the blisters and hearing my dad yell about the new dents in his now-no-longer-new truck. I didn't care, I was on a mission. In a typical teenager's world, there are only a few things that really matter.

There it was, a 1972 Corvette Stingray, the last year with the chrome bumpers. The timing was perfect. It was coming up on spring, and I had finally saved enough for my new baby. It was not just a car, it was my future. If Jamie liked me before, she would really like me now. We were gonna look good cruising the streets.

The interior was black and showed very little wear. The paint was shiny and the undercarriage was clean, obviously garage kept. It was perfect, my dream car. But only I could know that as I walked around it. My face had to be poker ready. The paper it was listed in had it for $7,500, a little more than it was worth at the time. So, despite my desire, I was intent on doing a little negotiating. I played it slow, asking some relevant questions about its history: where was it previously owned, what was its maintenance history, and so on. I then talked about the other ones I'd seen and their asking prices, not being too forward, just in a conversational way. My efforts were working. I could tell. Some of the beautiful folded bills in my pocket would never have to leave.

When the door of the tow truck slammed, I knew I was in trouble. There could only be one reason a tow truck would pull up to the same house I was at, in the back of some residential area.

"Are you, John?" the driver yelled to the guy I was talking to.

I didn't know his name, and I didn't care. My head was spinning. All cool I had was now lost. I could barely breathe let alone speak. I found my voice and forced out, "Who is that?"

But, before the seller could even finish telling me that he was some guy he'd spoken to earlier, my cash had exited my pocket and "I'll take it" had left my lips. You see, time was no longer on my side.

CREATIVE MARKETING

On the trips to Pennsylvania my family would take each year to visit my grandmother, I remember seeing a furniture store just off the highway at the exit to her house. It looked like every other store, except for the big "Going out of business" banner that stretched nearly the length of it. Which was not that unusual. But in all the years we visited, the store was still in business.

So the banner was really saying, "There is some serious savings going on here and it won't last long." The store's proximity to the highway always allowed for a new audience. The store's marketers, it seems, understood the benefit of time pressure.

OKAY, YEAH, BUT IS IT ALL JUST IN OUR MINDS?

Michael DeDonno, a researcher in the Department of Psychology at Case Western Reserve University, suggests that it's not just the *actual* pressure of time that affects our decisions, but the *perception* of time pressure as well. "If you feel you don't have enough time to do something, it's going to affect you."

Michael recently studied a group of students using a popular psychological assessment tool, the Iowa Gambling Task, to measure the effect of perceived time pressure.

It has been shown in research that *real* time constraints can adversely influence one's performance in certain skill based games. But Michael's goal was to determine the effects when there was just the *perception* of a lack of time.

The Iowa Gambling Task is a popular psychological test designed to simulate real life decision making. It is basically a game that determines an individual's ability to make a beneficial choice. It was introduced by Antoine Bechara, Antonio Damasio, Daniel Tranel, and Steven Anderson, researchers at the University of Iowa. In case you're not familiar with the Iowa Gambling Task, I'll briefly describe it here. It goes something like this:

A selected group is presented with four decks of cards. The participants are told that each time they choose a card, they will win some money. But in some cases, choosing a card may cause a loss. The objective is to attain as much money as possible. Each card drawn will either win a reward or inflict a penalty. As a result, some decks are "bad decks" and other decks are "good decks." The results of the study show that most healthy people are able to quickly determine which decks are the "good" ones. In as few as ten trials, the participants showed signs of stress when choosing from the "bad decks."

Michael DeDonno separated his subjects into two groups. The first group, the experimental group, was told that the time allotted to complete the test was inadequate. The second group, the control group, was told there was sufficient time to complete the task. Unlike previous tests, in which actual time pressure was measured, this study only measured the perception of time. The actual time given to both groups was the same, and it was quite sufficient for completing the task. The focus was shifted from how *actual* time pressure affects IGT performance to how *perceived* pressure affects it. DeDonno had his participants studied in two scenarios: one in which time was thought to be an issue, and one in which time was thought not to be an issue. In addition to both groups being given sufficient time, two of the groups were further broken down. One of them was given less time for the participants to make their decisions.

The results were that the participants who were told they had insufficient time performed significantly worse than those who were told they had enough time, regardless of the actual time allotted. In both cases, if they were told they had enough time, they performed better.

Michael DeDonno believes that this shows that time is relevant and must be thought of as so. He suggests that to better act or decide, we should try to focus on the goal, and not the time allotted. As he explains in his study, it is the perception of time that matters most. So while the decision-making process is inherently emotional, he suggests that you should first focus on ignoring the feeling of being rushed, and just focus on the task at hand.

PROCRASTINATION

Another result of time pressure is procrastination. In our time-pressured world, procrastination is the act of putting off a task or decision until a later time. In psychological terms, it is the act of replacing a higher priority action with a lower priority action.

There are generally two types of procrastinators. First, there are the people who are generally uncaring, whose inaction is mostly due to laziness. Then there are the people who are just more pressure sensitive. Their feelings may be more of indecision or panic, which can result in additional "stress" that further promotes procrastination.

The anxious are usually overwhelmed by pressure and are unable to gain a realistic sense of time. This causes stress and makes it difficult to focus on completing the task at hand. Many feel the need to relax first. Others may simply feel that they will be in a better state of mind to handle the decision at a later time. Both states, as you can imagine, lead to further procrastination. This cycle of delay can also have a debilitating effect on their personal lives and relationships. Overanalysis can often lead to paralysis. For the influencer, any attempt to induce a pressured decision is often detrimental. Before you can encourage a forward move, the person must first feel a sense of relief, or pressure release.

FAVRE IN THE FOURTH

The key idea in Michael DeDonno's study, I believe, is that to best perform, you should focus more on the task at hand than the pressure of the time.

Some, as we often get to see while watching any sport, are better at this than others. And some actually use it to their advantage. This is one of the factors that separate the gifted from the average. Have you ever noticed how some people fall apart under pressure while others thrive? The beauty of this is the opportunity it can create.

My favorite example is the "two-minute drill" in football. The sense of urgency in the last minutes of a close game is always guaranteed to create unparalleled excitement. The immediacy of the two minute drill heightens awareness and sometimes makes players exhibit abilities that seem to defy ordinary play.

Would you bet against Mr. Favre, Tom, Peyton, or Drew with two to go, and down by less than seven? Starting back on their own twenty; the energy on their side of the line and in every home with a TV is electric. It creates an adrenaline high that influences viewers to extreme degrees of desire and intent. No logical gambler could wager against it.

While most of us may be adversely affected by the influence of time pressure, not everyone is. Some people excel under pressure when others fold. Some are superstars in practice, and some are superstars when it really counts.

ALWAYS CREATE YOUR OWN PATH

Not everyone can excel under pressure, but everyone can increase their chances by understanding the influences that can and will affect their actions and the actions of the people around them. There will always be those who are better at responding than others. This is what separates the people who excel from those who do not. Another example of this can be seen in business.

The key to using influence to your advantage is to understand its positive benefits. All successful businesses use time pressure to their benefit. They thrive on being competitive. It is the businesses that can perform the best under pressure that succeed. Like superstars in the last minutes of a game, it is the companies that get their products out first while maintaining quality that are the most successful. If it were not for competition and the desire to be first, we would probably not have as many of the benefits that we do. Competition creates the desire in each of us for better and more affordable products. This is especially true in the ever-changing field of technology; but more and more, it has come to indicate success in any field. Time pressure helps to create the necessary energy to excel. Those who can perform under pressure will always rise above the rest.

The key to benefiting from any influence is in understanding its potential effects on you and your decisions and actions, as well as the effects it can have on others. For example, as a golfer on a final putt or a buyer in a showroom, you might seek to control your emotions. But as an opposing defense attorney or a salesperson in the field, you might prefer to create a sense of urgency. In each scenario, awareness and a plan can aid in your specific quest. Learn to control your emotions for the benefit of your own influence, and yet allow for the emotions of others to help create the influence you desire.

Athletes, desiring to be the best, may benefit from visualization exercises and forms of meditation. Marketers however are better suited to create an optimal balance of supply and demand and and create the pressure an expiration date will afford. In any case, as with any influence, there is always an opportunity. It is all in how you accept and adjust to the influences that decide your fate. Again, when the influence is time pressure, I believe Michael DeDonno said it best: Concentrate on the task at hand.

NOTES

Once interested, I felt compelled to take a look at Patty Hearst's own book, *Patty Hearst: Her Own Story*, New York: Avon. Although I was very young at the time and the news wasn't my main interest, I do remember the media's infatuation with her. After "living" much of her own book and the books of others, it's hard not to empathize with her and her situation. Her exemplary life since is an inspirational example to others in not letting a past experience negatively affect your future. Dateline NBC did a story as well, called "Kidnapped Heiress: The Patty Hearst Story," which can be found at msnbc. msn.com. William Graebner wrote *Patty's Got a Gun: Patricia Hearst in 1970s America*, Chicago: University of Chicago Press, 2008. Mr. Graebner did a very good job of engaging the reader and bringing certain scenarios to life. And for teaching us the methods of the "forced persuader," we have the *Saturday Evening Post* to thank, the April 1976 edition. When Benjamin Franklin first published the *Pennsylvania Gazette* in 1728, before it became the *Post* in 1821, I am quite sure, even as inventive as he was, that he couldn't have predicted its future website.

The first book I read about Adolf Hitler was *A Concise Biography of Adolf Hitler* by Thomas Fuchs, Berkley, 2000. I read it while sitting in Barnes and Noble. It was really nice of the employees to let me just hang around and read, free Wi-Fi too. I also read most of *Mein Kampf*, prepared by Ralph Manheim, Mariner Books, 1998. *Adolf Hitler: The Definitive Biography* was written by John Toland, Anchor, 1991. And *The Rise and Fall of the Third Reich: A History of Nazi Germany* was written by William Shirer, Simon and Schuster, 1990. Mr. Shirer's book is often a quoted resource.

For further reading on Jim Jones, I recommend *Raven: The Untold Story of the Rev. Jim Jones and His People* by Tim Reiterman and John Jacobs, Dutton, 1982. Also, *Seductive Poison* by Deborah Layton, Anchor, 1999. And a piece by Paul VanDeCarr called "Death of Dreams: in November 1978, Harvey Milk's Murder and the Mass Suicides of Jonestown Nearly Broke San Francisco's Spirit," the *Advocate*, November 2003.

Chapter 2: Placement

Time magazine published the article that was my main source for the "Placement" chapter. It was called "New York Blackout on July 25, 1977." It was set as a cover article. *How We Got Here: The 70's, The Decade that Brought You Modern Life—For Better or Worse* by David Frum, published by Basic Books, 2000, also provided a compelling history about the scenes and actions that took place. Ernest H. Wohlenberg, of Indiana University, wrote a piece, I think, just for my book. It is aptly titled, "The 'Geography of Civility' Revisited: New York Blackout Looting, 1977," copyright 1982.

Dr. Lawrence Sanna is known for the Better Decision Making Laboratory at the University of North Carolina. His studies can be found in many magazines and on the university's website at ncu.edu.

Dr. Sally Augustin is the author of *Place Advantage: Applied Psychology for Interior Architecture*. Her book is published by Wiley, April 6, 2009. I found it available on amazon.com. She also has a blog, "People, Places, Things," that I found linked to psycologytoday. com. Her website is designwithscience.com.

I first learned about Professor Kathleen Vohs and other interesting takes on the effects of sound from an article by Emily Anthes, published in *Psychology Today* on September 1, 2010. Kathleen Vohs is a professor of marketing at the Carlson School of Management at the University of Minnesota. She has a doctorate in psychological and brain sciences from Dartmouth University. She has also published over 130 articles and is often quoted for her expertise.

The work of Joshua Ackerman from MIT, Christopher Nocera from Harvard, and John Bargh from Yale, called "Incidental Haptic Sensations Influence Social Judgments and Decisions," includes a full-page list of people who have referenced their work. You can find a link to their study at sciencemag.org.

Researchers Arthur Aron and Donald Dutton are well-known for their research. Their study, often referred to as the "High Bridge Study," can be found in the *Journal of Personality and Social Psychology*, 1974. The high bridge in their study was the Capilano Suspension Bridge.

CHAPTER 3: RITUAL

The introductory story of chapter six on ritual and an obsessive nature is a compilation of many episodes of *Monk*. For a number of years, I was able to catch the episodes on the USA Network. Monk is one of my favorite characters. Because there's a possibility that we share some of the same traits.

The OCD Foundation is a reputable and active organization in Northeast USA. It is dedicated to helping the many people and families of people who suffer from obsessive-compulsive disorder. One of the most beneficial tasks that the foundation performs, in my opinion, is to help bring awareness to this disorder. Just as with the Innocence Project, the OCD Foundation is not for profit, and I believe its work is very beneficial. I am praying for a cure.

The theories and research of Dr. Burris F. Skinner can be found all over the Internet and in psychology literature. I found "Superstition in the Pigeon" in a review by Christopher Greene in a *Journal of Experimental Psychology*, published by York University, in Toronto, Canada.

CHAPTER 4: PAST EXPERIENCE

"How Past Experiences Inform Future Choices," published December 22, 2010, is the title of the research conducted by MIT researchers. The article can most easily be found from the website web.mit.edu.

Many good examples of profiling and stereotyping can be found at dictionary.com; in the historical standard; in the *Merriam-Webster Dictionary*, which can also be found online; and at encyclopedia.com. And, of course, Wikipedia.com is always helpful. It also lists many citations for the work shown.

The website adherents.com is a comprehensive source for information on many of our religions.

I think everyone has a goal in life. My goal is to one day write as well as Mr. Malcolm Gladwell. His books, including the awesome *Blink*, can be found just about anywhere, even in many homes all over the world. There is really nothing more to say. His writings speak for themselves, volumes.

CHAPTER 5: EMOTION

The *Report of the Independent Commission* on the Los Angeles Police Department is the main investigation of the LA riots. The commission was headed under Warren Christopher, which is why the report is called the Christopher Commission Report. It was unexpectedly thorough and very objective. Its view of the underlying causes and recommendations for the future were well received and appeared void of bias. Mr. Christopher went on to become secretary of state for President Bill Clinton.

An equally good book, by Lou Cannon, is called, *Official Negligence: How Rodney King and the Riots Changed Los Angeles and the LAPD*, Boulder, Colorado: West-View Press. Many specific details of the riots can also be found in "The L.A. 53," by Jim Crogan, published in *LA Weekly*, April 2002. Mr. Crogan was able to bring to light many of the final moments of the fifty-three people who died in the riots. After reading the article, many of their deaths seemed to be utterly random and senseless. "The Untold Story of the LA Riot," by David Whitman for *U.S. News & World Report*, published May 23, 1993, was also a compelling read, very street level.

I first read about Mrs. Yvonne Chevallier and her emotional predicament on the website of truTV.com, in a story called "Death in the Family." I followed up with an interesting website called murderrevisited.

blogspot.com. Both of these sites offered many stories of a surreal nature. True life, it seems, is often stranger than fiction. Yvonne's story is also part of David Buss's book, *The Murderer Next Door: Why the Mind Is Designed to Kill*, Penguin Press, 2005, which is available at amazon.com.

As I said in chapter one, my favorite article on revenge, titled "Sweet Revenge May be a Hard-Wired Reward," was written by Amanda Gardner, a *HealthDay* reporter. I found her article on news.healingwell.com. Other articles and reviews can be found at businessweek. com and the huffingtonpost.com.

I initially found Brian Knutson's view in a review titled "Sweet Revenge?" in *Science* magazine, published August 27, 2004. I have since found he is quite popular in "the study of the mind" and is often a quoted resource. As of this writing, he is a professor of psychology and neuroscience at Stanford and a significant researcher in the understanding of emotions and the decision-making process.

I first learned about the work of Dr. Jennifer Lerner while reading an article by Aimee Lee Ball in *O, The Oprah Magazine*. After some research, I soon found that her work is extensive and often quoted. Much of her work can be found on the Harvard Kennedy website. Entering content.ksg.harvard.edu in your browser should get you there.

Mr. G. Dep confessed as I was writing this book. I was actually typing while watching the TV. The Fuse network, mtv.com, and cbs.com are just some of the sources I regularly visit. Not sure if you know this, but the Fuse network still plays music videos. It also has entire blocks of featured artists. Lil' Wayne, it seems, is quite the businessman and marketer.

Miami's Nolan Carroll was also tripped as I was writing. I think ESPN followed up with quite a few views, certainly enough to include some of their reporting in my book. The websites nypost.com and cbs.com helped out with anything I might have missed.

CHAPTER 6: MOMENTUM AND COMMITMENT

The material on the influence of momentum and commitment is from the admirable website for the Innocence Project at innocenceproject.org. I believe there is no greater cause than freeing the innocent, and I thank them for their work. It is comforting to know that they have many extremely sharp individuals who believe in this cause. This site led me to the very compelling document "Emotionally Charged: The Prosecutorial Charging Decision and the Innocence Revolution" by Daniel S. Medwed, a professor at the University of Utah, and published in the *Cardozo Law Review*. The complementary research of Alafair Burke and her "Improving Prosecutorial Decision Making: Some Lessons of Cognitive Science," published in the *William and Mary Law Review* in 2006, was also quite influential. Her words were so well placed that it was difficult not to quote her.

Much of my understanding of the biases that can influence us can be found in the work of Keith A. Findley and Michael S. Scott in "The Multiple Dimensions of Tunnel Vision in Criminal Cases," 2006.

As a human being, I sincerely appreciate the efforts of all these people. At times, I was so entrenched in their writings that I actually lost sight of where I was with my own.

Some of the other biases I mentioned were referenced from a compilation of sources and my own knowledge. A good guide and further support for the biases I listed can be found in "26 Reasons Why What You Think is Right is Wrong" by Wade Meredith.

Chapter 7: Time Pressure

The Rogers commission report, at least much of it, is available online. Its full name for searching is *Report of the Presidential Commission on the Space Shuttle Challenger Accident*. The site I found it on was science.ksc.nasa.gov. I found individual volumes, which were often more complete, at history.nasa.gov. The premise of time pressure is rooted in chapter eight.

Michael DeDonno's work can be found on the Case Western Reserve University website at case.edu.